Fit *for* J⊙y

THE HEALING POWER OF BEING YOU

D1091637

Valeria Teles

Rowe Publishing

1 3 5 7 9 8 6 4 2

Published by

Rowe Publishing
www.rowepub.com

Dedication

To my mother -
She has taught me one of the hardest lessons in life:
that forgiveness and joy are inseparable.

Contents

Part Two

FROM FITNESS TO DEPRESSION

Part Three

FROM DEPRESSION TO JOY

Conclusion

LESSONS LEARNED

Final Reflections

Acknowledgments

Appendices

The End

Introduction:
Why Did I Punish Myself?

I went for a run because I had eaten a small, organic, dark chocolate cookie the day before and I felt that I had to punish myself. It was habitual for me to punish myself with strenuous, caloric compensation cardio whenever I felt guilty for enjoying life by eating tasty foods. When I placed first in a fitness competition, my fitness goals went up a notch. Winning the competition was one thing, but people complimenting me for my extra lean body pressured me to stay that way. I couldn't allow myself to look "bigger" again, and "bigger" really meant not seeing my defined ab muscles.

It was a sunny Sunday afternoon just after midday when I went for that run. Cresting a hill in the park, I came across a family outing. The adults were talking and laughing, and the kids were playing with a ball. They had bagels, cakes, sodas, and fried foods set around an improvised table. The family members were all overweight; some were even obese.

Out of breath from the incline of the hill, my body slowed but my thoughts sped up. *Look at them! These people should be ashamed of themselves. All fat, and they come to the park just to eat more fatty foods. They should be exercising, restricting their diets. How irresponsible.*

These judgments were quickly succeeded by a stream of thoughts that sprang up in my mind one after another, like weeds.

I don't like having to run; why did I eat that cookie?

I wish I had friends and family to be with right now.
My knee hurts; the brace isn't really helping.
It's too hot.
I don't like sweating this way; it messes up my hair.
What am I going to eat for dinner? There's nothing delicious to look forward to... I am sick of eating chicken and broccoli. But I have to; I won't be like these overweight people goofing off in the park. In this state of mind, I continued to run.

I worked endlessly to maintain the external appearance of health, but no one would have wanted to look like me if they knew the toxic mindset and true unhappiness that came with the abdominal six pack. My lifestyle lacked life; my body was tired, my mind had no clue it was causing its own suffering, and my heart wasn't there at all.

Had I died after that uphill run, my last wish would have been to trade places with those happy, out-of-shape people in the park. They were closer to what life is all about—love and kindness—even in overweight bodies surrounded by cakes and burgers.

* * * *

We focus so much on the pursuit of physical and mental health. We take our daily vitamins, eat healthily, exercise, sleep well, do our jobs to fulfill a sense of security and purpose, we search for comfort in romantic love, and travel for fun. We strive for happiness, for the most part, by engaging in pleasurable activities—sex, food, friendships, and future plans. We cultivate these habits to keep ourselves on a "healthy" track. I did so for years, although deep in my heart I doubted it was truly the path to achieve a healthy life as a human being. These unexamined habits seemed more like self-preservation and the perpetuation of established concepts and societal ideals than a real, authentic lifestyle.

Think about the word "healthy." Conventionally, it means to be well, fit, strong, and in good health. However, I question this definition. I have come to realize that a healthy person has a kind and gentle heart, regardless of his or her physical and mental health. Think of Gandhi and Mother Teresa. They both came close to death because of failing physical health, but they never stopped loving others. As for mental illness, my question to you is, do you believe a mind caught in the habit of expressing negative emotions is in a healthy state? It's easy to accept physical health as being free of injury or illness, but can we agree to define mental health as a condition of emotional well-being?

Unfortunately, most of us believe negative emotions are normal. Selfishness can give the illusion of success as we achieve materialistic accomplishments while being unkind to ourselves and everyone around us. In reality, behind selfishness lies insecurity, anger, and fear—especially of not having enough or feeling like we are not enough as individuals. Fear and anger trick us into agreeing with destructive ideas and actions simply because they are conventional, and insecurity builds mental barriers for protection. By acting and reacting to irrationality (fear), we reinforce our thinking mind's reality over that of our hearts. Even though these physical and mental states appear healthy to our materialistic perspectives, we must reject the normalization of negative emotions and behaviors like selfishness and fear.

After more than twenty years of participating in the fitness lifestyle, I realized a truth my heart had already mastered: a fit and healthy body comes second to a serene and loving mind. I wrote this book to explore the following questions:

- How can we integrate conventional fitness and spirituality?
- How do we exercise a healthy and joyful heart, despite a painful past?
- What does it mean to be truly healthy?

I do expect some of you to open this book, skip over the introduction, and start skimming to find exercise and diet tips. You have your own reasons for doing this, and I understand. You are probably enticed by the word "fit" on the cover, even though the word "joy" is bigger.

Yes, you will find exercise tips and diet suggestions here; and yes, they can help you get in shape if that is important to you. However, as a personal trainer, I was shocked to realize that physical fitness should not have become the priority it became in my life.

In working with clients, it became clear to me that they were forcibly engaging in exercise for reasons other than to supplement their already happy lives and "fit hearts." They—and I—were using exercise as a form of escape from a reality rooted in the fear of illness and death, in emotional pain, and in the struggle to find happiness and peace.

This was especially obvious to me when I worked with clients who had medical problems. Their lives were inauthentic and stressful, from their work to their personal relationships—again, not all that different from my own. The relationship they had with both exercise and with me as a trainer was hardly healthy. We were causing each other more pain by implementing exercise in our lives out of fear. This turned a potentially enjoyable activity into a torturous experience for all of us.

In *Fit for Joy*, I share how my relationship with the body, exercise, and food changed following a period of major depression. I lost interest in life amidst the most successful moments of my career, despite being in the best shape I had ever been in.

There was a strange inversion: The more I perfected my body, the sadder I became. I was working out well and found incredible success, but no amount of weight lifting lifted my spirit. When I won first prize in a bodybuilding competition, I became dangerously depressed. I had to touch bottom and seek wisdom and direction in order to heal, but I could not resolve this until I found answers within myself. I began to question the meaning of fitness and health, which led me to explore the depths of my own heart.

My soul-searching for true awareness and joy took me back to my birthplace: Brazil. There, exploring my childhood, I found the motivations that led me to Miami and New York. Along the way, I left the fitness industry behind and ended up in Paris writing this book. It was in Paris that I discovered the ancient wisdom and inner strength that has helped me throughout my journey.

I will show you how my suffering finally eased and suggest ways for you to find your own path to peace and joy.

In the beginning, I really thought I was listening to my heart by becoming a personal trainer. I wanted to help others achieve a healthy lifestyle. Although my life at that time seemed purposeful and happy, I was just another human being creating escape strategies and external ways to find meaning and peace—not very different from what my clients were doing.

Without a doubt, accomplishments and changes (such as winning first place in a fitness competition, leaving a long and painful marriage by divorcing my husband, and being in love again with someone new) were exciting and made me feel optimistic about life. These were all refreshing events that accompanied the beginning of my personal training career. However, my exciting new life was born out of stale thoughts based on dissatisfaction with a strong need to keep moving forward to justify moments of thrill.

To bring forth the importance of changing habitual patterns of the mind, I've arranged this book into sections. Each section describes a shift in my perspective in relation to physical fitness. Together, these sections encompass the before, during, and after of my continuing search for awareness. This sequence of events can help you see that everything is interconnected. The book begins with my early life experiences, moves into relationships mired in fear and pain, then explores the period in which I took refuge in fitness to ease emotional distress, and eventually leads to my professional involvement in the fitness industry as a professional trainer and competitor. Next, and finally, is the "dance" I had with a period of major depression, which led me into the depths of my own heart and toward solutions that were compatible, in fact drawn from my true spirit and illuminated by my new knowledge.

May the insights I gained help turn your physical existence into an adventure toward a life of serenity, kindness, and joy.

PART ONE

THE BEGINNING

Chapter 1

Early Trauma Sets the Stage for Later Distortions

The events listed in the passages below occurred from the ages of five to sixteen, and were the catalyst for a greater feeling of love and liberation through forgiveness and compassion. They are based on raw feelings that were attached to the memories of my early life experiences. Through them, I've learned to understand essential points: one is that our past is only a story; second is that we have the power to change our perception of ourselves and life; and third, that holding on to a negative state of mind can cause most of our unhappiness, addictions, and dissatisfaction. The answer was, is, and always will be love and kindness.

HOT PORRIDGE

We had just returned home from church.

"Your brother is hungry! Don't you see that?" she screamed from the other room.

I ran to the kitchen, a place I knew too well for my age.

The baby was crying. I was tense. She came to the kitchen, too. I felt her impatience and my spine seemed to tighten as she watched me.

I looked for the rice flour mix inside the kitchen cabinet. I could barely reach it. I remembered there was milk in the fridge... but where? Top shelf? It seemed to be hiding. I was so scared, I could not think...

It was important that I concentrate. I couldn't spill the milk or drop a spoon. A spilled drop of milk meant lots of salty tears spilling from my eyes, but it could get worse. They could be drops of blood from a painful pinch. Either way, I couldn't make any mistakes.

She was watching me. Her red-rimmed eyes blinked continuously. I tried not to look at her, but my memory was reproducing every blink of her eyes. With it came the sensation that I would become paralyzed any second, or worse, use more rice flour than necessary.

I had done this so many times before, but this day I felt like I didn't know what I was doing. The baby cried louder. In my head, her red-rimmed eyes blinked faster. Her impatient breath grew colder and colder around my spine.

I was afraid, but I could do it. While I was pouring the milk in the pan, I heard Aldo, the stray cat, screech in pain. He flew out the kitchen door just like a ball kicked to the goal on a soccer field. Poor cat. Even a ball would be luckier. At least it had a net to catch it. She was a great player of this kind of game, where the same team won over and over because they always picked a much weaker opponent to play against.

I heard the cat hit the ground hard. By then, I was shaking in fear. My eyes were filled with tears. I hoped the cat was not dead, but I couldn't help him. I couldn't even help myself. I promised I'd check on the cat later.

With shaking hands, I added the rice flour to the milk that was heating on the stovetop. The baby was crying louder and louder.

"Hurry up!" she screamed at me.

The cooking couldn't be hurried. I didn't know what to do. If I turned the flames up higher, it might burn the bottom of the pan. I didn't say anything, and I didn't look back. I felt like I was inside a box being shaken by a giant baby who didn't know how to play with his toys. There was nothing I could do about it. I felt like the poor cat. The only difference was he was a soccer ball, and I was a doll in a box. Both of us had no choice but to remain in a game we were destined to lose.

The porridge was bubbling, ready. It was very hot. I walked through the kitchen door, carrying it in the pan. I brought another empty pan with me. I looked for the cat, but he was nowhere to be found. I sighed with relief. He must be alive, somewhere far away from here.

I started to transfer the mixture from one pan to the other; I stood by the kitchen door where a fresh wind blew. The porridge needed to cool off before being poured into the baby bottle on the table.

She was looking at me impatiently while holding the baby. Overtaken by fear, I kept trying to cool off the hot food. I could barely breathe.

A few minutes later, I approached her with the pan. Mumbling the words, I asked her if it was cool enough to pour into the baby bottle.

The next thing I knew, I felt a burning sensation all over my face. The baby food had found a destination other than the bottle.

"Is that cool enough for you?" she shouted. "You can't do anything right. Here, hold the baby." She gave the crying child to me. "Let me handle it. Look what you've done! Now I've got to cook another one."

I could barely see. My baby brother was crying. I was crying.

I ran past the living room, placed the baby on the sofa—he was still too young to roll over—then ran into the bathroom. In the bathroom, I cleaned my face with cold water. I felt the cold water for a few seconds before I looked in the mirror. Then I looked and didn't recognize my face; it was red and swollen.

"Where are you?!"

I had to hurry. Tears were still rolling down my face. I dried them with a piece of a brown paper bag. There were plenty of brown paper bags in our bathroom; we couldn't afford soft toilet paper or paper towels. The brown paper was harsh on my skin, but not as harsh as the pain inside.

It was still early in the day, and I had so much work to do before the evening came. There was no time to cry. My tears would have to wait until I went to bed.

MY FAMILY

DARA was my mother. She was the only person in the whole world I endlessly wanted to please. There were no limits. She had all the power over me. Her demands were as sweet as fresh apples taken from a tree. They were golden opportunities that promised hope—delicacies sustaining my sense of existence.

A woman of Portuguese descent, she was the daughter of farmers from Bravo. My grandmother died when Dara was born. My grandfather quickly remarried so his new wife could help him take care of the kids, especially the newborn, Dara.

She was raised by her stepmother and older sisters. I heard she'd had a tough childhood. She constantly moved from house to house, where she was put to work as hard as an adult would have been. She found her way out of moving around by marrying my father. My father was dark-skinned, and he never made much money.

After having kids, Dara felt pressure to work extra hard to raise them. But making money to raise children wasn't the only motivation behind her efforts. Her abusive childhood motivated her to work, both out of fear and to gain love and attention, but it was also very important to her to prove that she could have a nice house, like her sisters.

I remember Dara going to visit one of my rich aunts every week. She had a large, comfortable, and well-furnished home, but my aunt didn't visit our house. I used to ask Dara why, and she would say that her sister was too busy working and taking care of her business and family. Her sisters had married their close relatives to join wealth, and they owned most of the shops in Bravo.

Dara used to work late nights making crocheted bedding and kitchen items to sell. She would save part of the money to increase the size of the house. Her obsession with having a large and comfortable home blinded her to the fact that a house without love and joy can never become a home.

JORGE was my father. He was short, physically strong, and walked with pride.

Jorge was a man who lived a simple, quiet life. I heard he used to dream about a better life. He aspired to become a professional musician like his older brother. Playing the accordion and singing was a passion that could have turned into gold if his rehearsals didn't start after an empty bottle of *cachaça*, a strong liquor made out of sugarcane. But his true adventures toward a better life began when he met Dara, my mother.

He married her when he was in his thirties. They moved from a small town to the big city of Sao Paulo, which was like the New York of Brazil, and right away my father "placed an order" for a daughter (me). He worked as a helper for a large and fancy resort, which hosted famous people and politicians. It was a beautiful place, surrounded by flowering bushes, rivers, tall trees, and many berry plants. My parents lived there for a while. They were given a place to stay in the back of the resort. Dara spent most of her days not only taking care of the house, but also learning how to swim and drive. For a small town girl, her individualistic interests had something to say about what she really wanted for her life; having children wasn't a wish but a "going with the flow" choice.

So I guess my parents didn't place an order for a baby girl, but rather accepted the package left on their front door. I was born at that beautiful resort, regardless. I remember enjoying fresh, sweet berries from the garden and riding in a boat with my father. My early "memory box" was filled with experiences with my father — not my mother—until a horrible event occurred. I was too young to remember the first tragedy of my life, for which I am grateful, as it would have been a brutal start.

My uncle Francisco, my mother's brother, also worked at the resort and used to live with us. One morning, he was found dead. Weeks after they broke up, my uncle's ex-girlfriend hired a hit man who murdered him as he was leaving for work. My mother said Uncle Francisco loved me dearly. He wouldn't leave the house without saying goodbye to me. Uncle Francisco has lived in my heart to this day. My mother's words about him turned into memories of love.

As for my father, most of the time I felt he was either trying not to see the world or wishing the world would not see him. For almost my entire life, my father was a mystery to me. His marriage to my mother was tense and felt unnatural. There were many unspoken words between them—especially about racism. My mother was white.

Dara's family didn't speak to Jorge. He was never there for birthdays, holidays, or any other kind of celebration that involved Dara's family. Everyone felt the tension, but no one talked about it.

Jorge didn't speak much. He seemed to be calm and cool all the time. Dara's family situation didn't seem to bother him. The image he presented was of a strong man who didn't owe anything to anyone and lived an anxiety-free life. Yet he seemed distant, and smoked and drank every day.

After we moved from the resort, he worked at a slaughterhouse and also on a plantation, growing food for us. Most of his days were the same. Jorge did what everyone did in his town: made enough money to live in a house, to eat, to buy clothes, and to buy a bike for short trips around town. He married and had children. From a distance, his life was simple and quiet, but when he picked up an accordion to play, he sang sad songs. I always wondered why he accepted his life the way it was if he wasn't happy.

ANA was my little sister. We were born a year and a half apart. Her rebellious attitude growing up not only got her into all sorts of trouble, it also shaped the way she looked. Her large brown eyes looked even larger when she became angry and frustrated about something. Her eyebrows came together when she found something strange, or didn't understand what others said or did—but the hair was her true trademark. Ana was often so busy bothering those around her that the comb could never find its way to the perfect destination. Ana's frizzy, curly, black hair was what you saw first when you spotted her. Her hair had a life of its own. Even if she hid behind a bush with dozens of black-feathered chickens, her hair would stick out. It grew upward and outward, never downward. It seemed to want to touch the sky and say hello to the moon. It could have been a good thing, but Ana disliked her hair enough to not care about it.

Ana would find ways to get attention by pestering others. She especially spent time making plans to annoy Dara. One method that usually worked was touching Dara's clothes with dirty hands. Dara would grow angry and get the belt.

However, sometimes Ana's plans to annoy Dara didn't work. One morning, after playing with mud, Ana came straight to Dara for a muddy hug. Dara turned around just in time, looked at Ana, and said, "Hey, Annie, your hair is almost hitting the ceiling. You know that clown's wig on TV? It looks just like that. Go fix it." Dara laughed out loud. She knew this was the only sure way to sabotage Ana's plan.

Ana ran to the bathroom and tapped and pressed her hair down nervously in front of the mirror. It never really worked. Shame took her by the ear back to her room. She moved slowly, keeping close to the walls of the kitchen and living room and looking to the sides to make sure no one could see her. She did a better job of sneaking than any detective who spots an unguarded fugitive buying fruit at a street market.

In her room, she would quietly hold her doll in her lap. She combed the doll's hair, which was perfectly straight, smooth, and long. Ana dressed and undressed her doll many times. The doll had more clothes than she did. Half of Ana's clothes were torn into pieces to make dresses for the doll. This was Ana's pastime when she couldn't annoy Dara. She was not happy playing with her doll. I have a feeling that Ana didn't really want to cause trouble. Deep down, she just wanted a warm hug from Dara. I guess Ana and I had the same wishes with different ways to fulfill them.

THE TOWN

I grew up in an inland town named Bravo, in the state of Bahia in Brazil. Bravo was unlike the coastal towns and cities, which are nestled in next to the blue tropical sea, adorned with flowers, and fringed with waving palm trees. Bravo is not one of Brazil's famous resort places like the Coconut Coast or an exciting center like Sao

Paulo. Bravo is dry most of the year, a parched place where only the people who were born there and cannot dream of leaving remain. It is three hours from the capital, Salvador, and even further from anywhere you might wish to be.

The best that can be said of Bravo is that it is an unpretentious place, and it assumed the loyalty of its native inhabitants. Bravo is not on any tourist maps, and even today, there are no "Recommended Places to Eat" or "Sights to See."

Its narrow, unpaved streets didn't want to be more than what they were. The vegetation was grateful when seasonal rains revived the landscape. Even the grass, which died before this glorious bath, didn't complain about how hard it was to live; it was simply living the life it was meant to live, neither happy nor unhappy, but alive. In the 1870s, the dry seasons extended for so long that many people starved in this region during great famines.

But even Bravo can look to lusher, more vital places, and my eyes were drawn to the distant mountains that surrounded us. Those mountains were dark green; they smiled at me from a distance. I smiled back. The humble brick houses, most of them unfinished, matched the town's spirit of simplicity and openness. These houses would be painted one day, as the streets would also one day be paved, but no one expected anything too good or too soon. There was a small, garden-like square in the center of town, with some tall trees and flowers. I often walked through there when I needed to run some errands. Couples met there—I saw them as I walked by and wondered what they talked about.

Bravo's dusty roads were still paths for bull-driven carts and carriages, which squeezed between the houses in a cloud of dust. The carriage driver would scream loudly to give directions to the bulls. He wore leather pants and a leather jacket under the fierce sun and whipped the bulls with two dirty ropes. From far off, I could hear the loud creaking of the carriage's dry wooden chassis carrying large bags of beans and corn.

The sound grew louder and louder as the carriage approached our street. It was a bit scary at first, but it always became the attraction of the week. I would rush to the window, covering my eyes with my fingers so as not to be blinded by the dust. I couldn't open my mouth to laugh or scream either, unless I wanted to have dust for lunch.

I still enjoyed the passing of the giant, creaking carriage, dragged by bulls and whipped by a wild man. Bravo seemed not to care about its bull-driven carriages making loud noises and clouds of dust. It was simply the space that allowed a bull to be a bull and a man to be a wild conductor.

WORK 'N LIGHT

My bedroom was very small with no door and no lights; we used an improvised kerosene lamp.

It was very hot in the summer and very cold in the winter because the roof was made of old tiles with lots of gaps. The nightly ritual before going to bed was always the same. I smashed a bunch of mosquitoes trapped in my old net, and let some lucky ones escape by lifting it. Then, I stitched over new holes to prevent them from coming in to bite us during the night. Even if they didn't get inside the net, their noise and Ana's extra warm hugs kept me from falling asleep sooner than I would have liked. She was too close and too touchy, enough to make me feel uncomfortable. Most of the time, I would send her away but sometimes, her hugs helped me fall asleep, even in scalding hot evenings.

Besides the mosquitoes and Ana's flaming arms, there was another problem I faced at night: the nightmares. They were always the same. It was dark; I was lying in bed and someone was coming toward me. I didn't know who it was, but I knew they were going to harm me. I couldn't move from my bed. I screamed in despair, trying to move. I couldn't. I woke up terrified. It was hard to fall asleep again.

The morning was my best friend. It brought just enough light to chase the darkness of my fears away. The thoughts of my next chore offered comfort. The housework made me smile. There was no fear or sadness anymore when I was working. It all vanished. It felt like listening to a beautiful song during every task. I giggled and smiled very often while I did them.

Work was my other best friend.

WATER CARRIER

Walking the path on my way to the river was such a gift to me. I liked seeing the dust lift around every step I made, as I dragged my worn-out sandals in the soil and swung my old gray bucket. My body had so much space to move; I loved the sensation. The late morning was silent, aside from my own giggling when I suddenly saw an animal cross the road.

I reached the river. I felt unconditional love there. It let me smile as often as I wanted. Before I started filling my bucket with water, I played by swiping my hands from side to side in the water. There were lots of small fish—they were close to the edge and not scared of me. I wondered if they were asking for help. Were they trapped? If so, I understood them.

The river was drying up. It would soon have no life to give to the fish, and it wasn't Mother River's fault. She couldn't give what she didn't have. The river and the fish were a family that stayed together for a while, and then would naturally grow apart.

I could have stayed there all day long playing with the water, but I needed to push the fish and the algae out of the way with my pink, scratched plastic cup and fetch water to fill my thirsty gray bucket. Then I placed a pre-rolled towel upon my head, rounded into a cushion to fit the bucket.

I carried the full bucket to the nearest large rock, where I squatted down in a level position and carefully placed the bucket on top of the towel on my head. At first, it was like being pressed down to the ground by the finger of a giant; but as I stood, everything felt normal.

I learned the technique of water carrying from an old, experienced water-carrier I'd met at the river. It was a lesson she was happy to teach me. She said there weren't many people she could teach those days. They were impatient and would rather carry the bucket of water in their hands.

Walking back home while balancing the bucket was fun. The woman told me that carrying the water on my head would feel much lighter than carrying the water any other way.

She also said something I didn't understand.

"You don't ever need to learn how to swim. If one day you fall in the water, don't be afraid. The water will remember you used to carry it on your head. It won't let you drown, because it wishes to be closer to the sky again through a water-carrier like you."

THE SUNNY DISHES

It was time for lunch. My stomach couldn't have been happier.

When I finished lunch, my other job started. I needed to fully concentrate on the task ahead: a sink full of very dirty dishes and a pile of pans with inches of thick food stuck to the bottom. There was a high price to pay if I broke a plate or dropped a spoon on the floor. This couldn't happen. It was a tough job, but I had to believe that I was tougher.

My feet and hands were large for my size. Maybe they grew longer to help me with all the work. The dry skin of my hands felt like an old woman's hands and looked like the cracked, dry land of the town. I made a firm agreement with my hands not to drop or break anything, or else the rest of my body would crack, too. It was a serious task. The dirty dishes and pans became the most important mission to accomplish on Earth.

Nothing could distract me from making every plate shine as bright as the sun's rays coming from the tiny window above my head. It helped me concentrate when I imagined them dry and shining in front of me. The shining dishes were beautiful to my eyes and calming to my mind. I emptied the sink and filled it with enough water to wash the bigger pans first. My hands were touching the water, picking up each dish, swiping every little bit of food with the sponge. I was precise.

At that moment, I was only a dishwasher. I, the sink, and the pile of dirty dishes were one. My mission was to clean them, but by the end I felt they had cleaned me, too. My breathing was lighter and I could smile freely. The water, the sink, the dishes, and the walls around me were occupied enough being themselves—they allowed me to be only the dishwasher.

Before I finished washing the dishes, I heard Dara's voice. It frightened me.

"Hurry up! You need to sweep the floor next, then take care of Justina. She needs you," Dara screamed from a distance.

Justina was my grandmother, my father's mother. I brought a hot lunch and dinner to her every day. She couldn't cook her own food anymore.

I had to finish cleaning the dishes as quickly as possible without losing my concentration. Anxiety was trying to take over. The vision of shining dishes helped me focus again.

A few minutes later, my mission was accomplished.

THE BUS

I heard Dara call me again. "Hurry up. It's getting late."

My heart was racing. I had to find the broom quickly.

It was early afternoon. I was tired already. There was another task of the day I had to do: sweep the floor. The broom was always hiding behind the kitchen door. That day, for some reason, it wasn't there.

I was scared of the broom. Its bristles brushed away the dust from the floor really well, but its tall, hard body was quite often used to take my smile away. I wished it didn't have a body, only bristles.

It was time to go outside to look for it.

There it was, by the chicken perch.

I went straight to the front window by one of the bedrooms. I always started there. It had a view of the main road leading out of the town. Buses and cars didn't come and go frequently, but the wait was worth it. I waited for them a few minutes. I used to daydream by that window for a while before sweeping the house. When I would see a bus was leaving, my heart jumped with happiness. I imagined myself inside that bus. It was taking me somewhere. I didn't know the destination, but it didn't matter. What made me smile was that I also imagined going to meet friends who loved me as I loved them.

"Hurry up." I heard her voice again.

The bus would disappear on the horizon quickly. It was a sad moment. A happy me was inside that bus, and it was leaving the sad me behind. I sighed.

I started sweeping the living room. It was a small space with a few pieces of old furniture, but there was one thing there that seemed new to me every time I looked at it: a large painting of a woman in water.

The painting was very important to Jorge. He often looked at the woman the same way I looked at the bus out of the window. He must have been imagining himself in that painting somehow. He closed his eyes for a brief moment in front of the painting, then calmly walked away. I took some time there to look at it, too.

The painting was of a woman who stood with a serene look on her face, even though she was in the middle of a stormy ocean. There were many bright stars and a glowing moon above her head. She was tall, beautiful, and had black hair. Her long white gown merged with the water. I didn't know if the water was coming from the woman or if the woman was coming from the water. It was hard to tell.

Her arms were relaxed and open, and she was dropping some seeds. The seeds became white blooming flowers even before they fell in the water. I wondered what kind of seeds they were. They were not the same as the ones I sowed with Jorge. White flowers don't make me hungry as beans do; they make me smile. But what I liked the most about the painting was how calm the woman was, despite being surrounded by the fierce ocean.

I needed to hurry. Justina was waiting for me.

JUSTINA

I was ready for my next mission—taking food to my grandmother, Justina. She lived about ten minutes away. I was leaving the house on Jorge's bike.

Getting the bike to move at first was not easy. It was heavy, and I was already sweating. My little sister, Ana, was on the back seat just for fun. She was adding extra weight I didn't need, which wasn't so much fun for me. The two bowls of hot food were inside my bag, hanging from the handlebars.

The rusty chain slipped off with my first attempt to move. I asked Ana to step off so I could put it back in place. It took a little while, and my hands were greasy and dark by the time I got the chain back on.

Ana jumped back on the backseat, and I finally got the bike moving properly. The tires moved slowly. There was too much weight, but with my mission in mind, nothing could stop me.

The town's roads were dusty and dry. The houses along the way were as sad and poor as the people in them. Everyone moved slowly on the streets—not much different from the bike. It could have been the scalding sun embracing them a bit too tightly. I encountered the same scene every time I took food to Justina.

I wondered if it would be different if I were to ride the bike on my own, without the extra weight and without a destination. I was often tense and in a hurry. Would everything around me look happier? Would I be smiling? I thought so. Just me, the bike, the dusty roads, and the wind on my face, nowhere to arrive or to go back to. It would be nice not to have a mission to accomplish, at least for a moment.

Justina was in her eighties. She was a small, grumpy lady. Her sunburned, dark, indigenous skin showed a lifetime of outdoor labor. The sun seemed to have kissed her for years in the fields. I was sure she had let the cool shade of the trees wait for her in vain. I'd heard she had fought for basic survival when she was a girl.

She lived alone and smoked pipe tobacco that she made herself. Her husband had died long ago, while she was still young—young enough to have married again, but she'd decided to be on her own instead.

Justina didn't talk much. When she did, she complained or said things I hardly understood. It was either about those parts of her past that she still remembered or because of a recent offense, though Justina always looked a bit sweeter when I arrived with her food.

I smiled while I watched her eat the hot meal. She tried to hide the shadow of a smile that struggled to come to life from the pleasure she felt as she ate. Her body was trying to speak, but her mind was still complaining about everything. The thoughts in her head didn't leave her alone for a moment.

Ana was bored and sat close by, pretending to play with an old straw hat lying on the floor. She asked me to hurry up Justina's meal, but I wouldn't do that. I waited patiently. When I came alone, Justina relaxed more. We had strange conversations.

I listened to her complain about everything and made my own silent comments. She grumbled about the house, the past, the stray cats that visited her place at night, the dogs crossing the street, the heat, and on and on. She even complained about the tobacco smoke coming out of her own mouth. Her anger intensified when the smoke made a cloud in front of her eyes so she couldn't see anything. Her hands swung back and forth as she tried to clear her vision.

I often asked myself, "Does she realize that she is making the smoke that is clouding her vision?" I can't help her with the smoke, because she will always make more. I wish I could help her stop making smoke.

Justina's tiny house was a bit scary, but I grew used to it. It was made of mud, not cement or bricks. It felt like the walls and the roof could fall at any time. It was dark, too. There were only a few pieces of furniture, and every single piece was covered with dust and spider webs. Everything smelled like tobacco smoke. I didn't know why she had an old stove—she didn't cook—but I guess she needed it to make her coffee and light up her tobacco pipe.

Visiting Justina inspired mixed feelings in me. Watching her eat made me happy, but I was saddened by listening to her complain about things she could change.

I waited until she finished eating, then put the empty containers back in the plastic bag and said goodbye. She never said goodbye to me. Farewells seemed to be tough on her. I wondered why. Maybe what she really wanted was to be around others, but they made her sad, so she chose to be alone. I wondered if it was better to be alone than to be around others and feel sad.

I believed Justina only regretted her decision to be alone when visitors came. We reminded her that she could have allowed a little joy into her life by being among others, even if they were a sad bunch.

Leaving Justina was a melancholic departure—a cold moment under a hot, clear, sunny sky.

On the way back, the streets and the houses were still sad; Ana was still heavy in the backseat.

But there were heavier things I would rather not carry.

WORKING FOR A HUG

It was late afternoon, and I was tired. It had been a long day, but there was still some corn shucking to do.

Before I started that task, I asked Dara, "Can I have a hug?" My tearful voice echoed through the room.

"Go do your work. I have a lot of things to do. I need to ensure you have a house, a bed, food, and clothes," she replied sternly.

"But you can still hug me," I insisted. I was afraid my request would be denied once again.

Dara mumbled and moved away, shaking her head as if I were asking for something that was not possible.

I would do the work without her hug. Maybe after I was done, she would reward me.

While shucking the corn, I watched from a distance as Dara hugged my cousin, who was about my age. Dara could see me looking at her from across the room. *What have I done wrong not to deserve a hug like my cousin?* I thought to myself. *I know she is prettier than me, but she doesn't work as hard as I do for Dara.*

Before I got back to my work, tears started to fall. I couldn't control them. They ran from my cheeks to my flowery dress. The flowers on my dress distracted me for a moment. They were so colorful. I could see them smiling at me.

I felt a bit better. I stopped crying and got back to my work.

Later that day, when the work was done, I went to sleep without my hug. But as long as I had work to do the next day, there would be lots of hugs to dream about.

JUST LOOK UP

It was getting late. The kitchen was clean—we'd had dinner not long before.

Everyone was already in bed when I quietly exited the kitchen into the dark. I took a few careful steps, hardly able to see where my feet were going, but I had done this so many times that my body would be guided by the clear purpose of my heart. It wanted a moment to itself. It was time to visit my "alley family."

That particular day, I had been very busy; my body ached and my mind wondered when all this would be over.

The alley I headed to was dark and muddy, but it didn't scare me. It was a narrow, tight passage alongside the house. It was the only place I could really be alone at the time. I was going there to have an unusual conversation.

I tried to fit my small body along the cracked, rough wall. There was a crooked metal fence on the other side, and I had to be careful not to get hurt.

Between the wall and the fence, I felt comfortable. The narrow strip of dry land close to the wall just barely accommodated my feet. I breathed and said to myself, *Just look up.*

When I looked up, I forgot where I was, who I was, where I had been, or where I needed to go. The view was one of silent magic.

A feeling of happiness and comfort arose in me right away. The sky, the moon, and the stars felt like a real family to me. I often asked myself, why couldn't I be up there with them? I really would have liked that.

There was no answer to my question, but I could feel that the stars were listening to me.

A VOTE FOR A TOOTH

It was Saturday morning—a street market day. This was when small farmers and vendors came from the mountains to the town to sell goods—mostly food.

People milling around. Colorful fruits and vegetables, ice cream stands, chickens and pigs for sale or trade, and birds singing in cages. This was also a day I worked less.

But this specific Saturday was different. Besides the street market, politicians were also promoting their election campaigns, and I was going to the dentist. Everything seemed related.

The town appeared to have been showered with paper rain. On these papers, I saw older men wearing serious clothes—black and white suits—and trying to smile while holding a stiff pose. These were the politicians on their election campaigns.

The songs they played were not fun. I heard the same songs over and over all day long. They were so loud I couldn't hear the birds anymore. Often, I caught myself singing along to these songs I didn't like. I wondered how it was possible to do something you didn't want to, and only realize it when you were already in the middle of it.

A few weeks before, my mother had made an awful deal. An adult family member told Dara my tooth was not good and that it should be fixed. Dara took me to a dentist. I got really scared by the noise the machine made and ran away from the place.

Later, one of the campaigning politicians sent some people to talk to Dara and they offered another option to fix my tooth. They said it would be fast and painless, that I wouldn't even hear any noise from the machine. All I had to do was close my eyes for a few seconds, and the bad tooth would be gone. And even better, the treatment was free!

Dara was very happy, and it meant a lot to me to see her happy. The politician's people wrote something on a sheet and Dara signed it. I was scared, but to see Dara smile I would do anything.

It was about noon. I walked alone across town, holding a small piece of paper with a long number written on it in my hand. Dara had given me directions. She told me to give the piece of paper to the dentist when I got there.

I understood it all, except for one question I kept asking myself, *Why am I walking alone to this place?* But even if I had an answer to my question, it wouldn't matter. Fear was destined to be my only companion that day.

I was as scared as I'd been before, with the first dentist and his noisy machine. But I'd made a promise, so instead of running away from what scared me, I walked toward it.

As I walked through the town, I felt there was nothing that could change the voice of fear in my head. The crowded, festive, and colorful streets didn't distract my thoughts. I wished I could catch myself singing that annoying song. For once, I wouldn't have minded.

It didn't take long to get to the dentist's office. I opened a red door and entered a tiny room. The lighting was dim and there were a few broken chairs. The place seemed to need more fixing than my tooth. An old lady sat behind a table.

That table is probably from my school. I sit behind one just like it, I thought. I crossed the room in front of the lady to sit in the back. There was another door behind her where the dentist worked.

The woman had frizzy gray hair and used glasses. She didn't smile at anyone. Her teeth probably needed fixing, too. I hoped she had an alley like mine. The sky family would make her smile freely, as much as I did. They didn't mind anyone with bad teeth. I had tested this out.

My thoughts strayed from fear for a moment while I thought about how the sky made me feel.

When my attention returned, the woman was looking at me. She was holding a pen and a sheet of paper. She asked my name. I gave her the paper in my hand, and she sent me back to my seat. It didn't take long before I heard another child scream.

What would happen to me there? The last sound I wanted to hear was my own name. I knew the lady would say it when it was my turn. Why did I have a name, anyway? I didn't need one. The sound of my name always scared me to the bone, especially at home. I guess it could have been worse. If I didn't have a name, people around me would use something else to frighten me. They did anyway, but at least the fear warned me before I felt the pain on my body.

A moment later, the woman looked at me again. Our eyes met, but we didn't say anything to each other. Why was I not running away from this place like before? This was so much worse than the first dentist I was taken to.

I know the reason: I'd made a promise to my mother. I gave her my word, so I had to stay until the end.

The lady called my name. I wasn't sure how I was going to get inside the other room. My legs were like jelly, my stomach hurt, and I was probably pale as a ghost. I couldn't speak a word. But I managed to get up from the chair and walk slowly toward the other room. The dentist, a tall man who didn't seem to notice how frightened I was, asked me sit on a strange high chair. It was scalding hot outside, as always, but all of a sudden, I felt very cold. My body was shaking. The tall man looked calm and cool. He didn't know I was about to pass out from fear.

He probably thought I was a strong and courageous girl to come alone for a tooth extraction. So I acted like there was nothing to be scared of. *Since nobody believed in my fear, why should I?*

This thought calmed me. Then I heard some metallic noises coming from behind the chair I was sitting in. There was also a strange smell in the air. This was not going to be fun, but I was prepared to be strong.

The combination of the smell, his silence, and the fearful thoughts trying to take me over again made me think of one word: torture.

What have I done? I asked myself. *I made a promise,* I answered. But I didn't know I would feel like a mosquito trapped in a bed net.

The dentist started to walk toward me, holding a large needle in his hands. He said nothing. My body was still shaking. It was getting colder and colder in there.

Then, instead of asking the dentist what he was going to do to me, I started a strange interrogation. "How old are you? Do you like working here? Did you buy some fresh fruit at the street market today?" I asked one question after another.

His only answer was, "Open your mouth wide, young lady."

At that point, I knew I was in serious trouble. He didn't want to talk and I couldn't talk. I had no choice but to pretend I didn't mind not knowing what was about to happen.

He came closer and closer. The warmth of his body made me feel like I was inside of a tight box. There was a sharp, brief pain that crossed my mouth to the back of my head. I couldn't do anything. *It has to end at some point.* This was the only thought in my mind.

Soon, my whole mouth felt heavy. Everything had been numbed—my gums, my lips, my fears, my thoughts, my body, my whole life. There was no other feeling left but surrender.

It wasn't over. Minutes later, he returned with a larger instrument. I was already paralyzed, but I wished my thoughts were paralyzed, too.

He asked me to open my mouth again. I heard a muffled sound that reminded me of a piece of glass being smashed, as if the glass had been wrapped up in a cloth and soaked in water so the sound didn't get too loud. There was no pain, but the numbness was its own kind of discomfort.

It didn't take long to see my tooth, lying in a tray by my side. I tasted blood. My tongue was searching for my tooth uncontrollably. She had lost part of her family. There was nothing I could do to comfort her. She wouldn't stop searching for it, the way a mother hen searches for her chicks who have died and had their bodies taken away from the roost.

The dentist's silence was now my silence. He had accomplished his mission. As for me, for the first time, I didn't have one, except to endure and overcome deep fear. I guess I did a good job of that.

For the next few hours, my mouth felt detached from the rest of my body—a strange sensation I yearned for once the pain arrived to spend a sleepless night with me.

The mosquitos trapped inside my bed net celebrated my absence. My alley family would wait for me in vain that night.

A SUNDAY MASS

Sunday morning. Dara, Ana, and I were climbing the steps to get to church. Each step I took felt lighter and lighter. The song that was playing inside the place made me feel different.

We reached the top. A woman wearing a red dress entered church, distracting all of us. After crossing the large door, the air seemed limited. It didn't allow me to breathe much of it. My whole body became sort of numbed, just like my mouth at the dentist. I couldn't be what I thought I was; a simple human being with healthy lungs that kept me alive. It was as if the air asked me not to breathe it. The music asked me not to move with it. The silence demanded more silence, and the image of a man on a cross demanded that I stop thinking.

We found a place to sit. I felt strangely fine. My body couldn't move because it was seated. When I was walking toward the bench, it felt like I was not supposed to be moving, although I had to.

The man wearing a long, white dress started to talk. Why did he speak in a melancholic voice? I didn't understand anything he said. Dara was next me—she seemed to understand everything. She held a booklet in her hands. She was reading the man's words there.

The place commanded silence, but my thoughts couldn't be silenced. They kept changing by the second with every image, smell, or sound I heard.

On my left side, there was a boy. A fly was sitting on his forehead. The man in the white dress was saying something I should have been listening to, but as long as that fly sat on the boy's head, my thoughts were with him. It felt to me like a problem to solve. How could I chase the fly away from his forehead without moving or talking? I didn't know.

The boy was more paralyzed than my mouth after all the injections. Didn't he feel something unusual on top of his skin?

That bothered me so much. I was getting impatient and uncomfortable. I heard someone whispering something from the front seat.

"Look at her. Doesn't she know this is the house of God?"

Was she talking to me? I hoped not. I was quiet. She couldn't be listening to my thoughts. Even my breath was shallow and controlled.

The whisper continued. "How can she wear a red dress to Church? This is the house of Jesus. She will burn in hell."

I didn't know what was wrong with the color red. I liked it. What did "burn in hell" mean? Red reminded me of fire. It was painful to be burned. But I did enjoy corn on the cob grilled on the bonfire. I liked the color red, and I liked the fire. I wondered what hell had to do with any of that. A bonfire that grilled women in red? What about people who whispered in Church about women in red? Would they be burned too? It all sounded too complicated for me.

I tried to stretch my neck to look at Ana, who was sitting next to Dara on the other side, but I couldn't see her.

A familiar smell traveled to my nose. It grabbed my attention. I recognized the smell very well. My father drank *cachaça* all the time.

I looked behind me. There was a man with grey hair wearing a black hat sitting close to me. He was looking down. He was either trying to fall asleep or he was sleep-talking. The man was nodding his head with every word the man with the melancholic voice said. He was repeating the words. He seemed to understand and agree with everything too, just like Dara.

Did they really understand the words of the man in white? Or did they just repeat them because it was all they could do?

I preferred to remain in my thoughts rather than to repeat words I didn't understand.

The mass was about to end. I knew because some people were forming a line to get closer to the man upfront. Dara got up and went up front too.

The music picked up. It was happier than the music that was playing at the start. The man was giving everyone something. He was putting it directly in their mouths. It was small and white—a circular, biscuit-like something. It might have been a candy, perhaps a sweet treat. I would have liked one, but I didn't see children going there. The solemn way the people acted when they bit the biscuit made me realize it was something sacred, perhaps a magical biscuit?

The music played louder and happier. I wanted to get up and dance.

It was not going to happen. There was a feeling of melancholy everywhere. After eating one of those white biscuits everyone walked extra slow and looked sadder than before. How come? Happy music and a biscuit should make anyone cheerful. I didn't understand the place.

I looked to my left. The boy still looked like a stone. The fly had found a permanent home on his forehead. I had to do something.

There was a brochure next to me, the one my mother was reading. She had left it on her seat to get a biscuit. That was it.

I started to fan myself as fast as I could. I pretended my left side was warmer than my right. The boy looked at me, oblivious, and the fly went away.

Whew—it was a relief that made me happy. He would never know he had a fly on his forehead during the entire mass, and that the left side of my face hadn't been overly warm at all.

The fly would find another forehead to rest on, no doubt. Too bad I wouldn't be there to fan it away again.

The mass ended. Dara, Ana, and I slowly stood and walked toward the large front door.

There were many other smaller doors on the sides of the Church, and I wondered why everyone left by the main front door, which was crowded, and exiting through any of those side doors might lead us where we want to be.

That Sunday, I returned home to experience another outburst of violence: My mother shouted and slapped me. Again, I was "too slow," a disobedient girl. I did not move fast enough for her, and whatever I did, I made mistakes. What did I do this time? Set the table? Carry another plate of food?

The plate fell to the floor of its own volition. My hands were trembling. I was crying before my mother even screamed and slapped my face and called me names. And deep in my heart was a more profound sadness: My mother had gone to Church; she had prayed; she had sung. She had even taken the sacred biscuit. But she had not changed a bit.

That was when I realized that just as they had all crowded together to exit from the one main door, most people emerged from Church exactly the same as they went in. My mother followed the crowd. Did she believe the man in the white dress? Did she hear messages of love and kindness? Apparently not. She was the same furious mother, and I was the same sad, wounded girl.

Chapter 2

Learning About Friendship

SOFIA

I was about thirteen-years-old when a stranger came to town and landed in our living room. Her long, black hair covered most of her face, hiding her large, kind eyes. She was a stranger with a familiar presence. There was curiosity in her eyes, and her shy smile didn't seem to belong to her face—as though her smile didn't want to be there at all. She looked sad.

I was hiding behind the table, looking at her and listening to the uncomfortable conversation she was having with my parents.

Her name was Sofia.

She came from a large coastal city many hours away. Daisy, my cousin, had asked her to come to support her return.

My parents adopted Daisy ten years ago, when she was only two-years-old. She was my uncle Francisco's daughter. When he died, her mother couldn't take care of her, so my parents did. She had run away some years back. No one knew what had happened to her until the day she showed up with Sofia.

Daisy's first job had been housecleaning for Sofia's mother—that's how they met. Beyond that, I didn't know much about Daisy or her life. We were never close growing up. Perhaps she was too busy with work to stay around and play with me. Before Daisy ran away, I did much less work. I remember feeling inspired by her courage to go away the way she did, although I thought it was not wise because she didn't have any money or a high school degree.

From where I was, I could see everyone and hear everything, but they couldn't see me. At least I thought they couldn't, but Sofia did. She got up from the sofa and walked toward me. My heart was beating fast. I was a nervous, frightened girl.

"What is your name, hiding girl?" she asked in a firm voice.

My tongue was so used to not talking that it took long naps sometimes. I could never wake it up on time to answer questions promptly, if at all.

"What are you doing behind the table? Come out and talk to me."

I really wanted to say something before she went away. My tongue was still asleep in the warm, comfortable space left by one of my teeth. Worried that Sofia might leave, I stared at her, looking deep into her eyes. I must have looked like one of those fish in our river, but I believed my eyes could communicate.

It was weird, I knew, but there was nothing else I could do. Talking wasn't happening. I felt like someone who had been held hostage for many years, and this was finally my chance at freedom. But I had to be cautious.

I kept looking at her intensely. I guess it worked, because she didn't go away. Instead, Sofia sat close to me in one of the chairs, and started to talk about herself.

She began talking about the place she came from, a city called Salvador that was close to the ocean and miles away from Bravo. I wondered if the ocean was the same salty water that came from my eyes when I was sad.

She said that she worked for a large company and that she sat behind a tall table—much bigger than the one in our house. All day long she sat there and gave people information about the company.

"Yes, I can tell that talking is something you do really well, Sofia," I tried to tell her with my eyes. I started to admire her.

She kept talking about her city and her work. I listened and made eye contact. My tongue still rested.

After a while, Sofia changed the subject completely.

"I am really sad right now. My heart is broken into so many pieces," she said. "I love him so much. He says he loves me, too, but he can't stay with me. He can't marry me. I don't know what to do." I heard tear drops in her voice. She lowered her head and went silent.

All of a sudden, my tongue woke up. Words rushed out of my mouth seemingly before I could think them, as if they had a life of their own, detached from my body and mind. Each word seemed to know what Sofia needed to hear. I started talking about love, joy, hope, faith, courage, and how strong we must be. That we should never give up on love, ever! I spoke with a passion I didn't even know I had until that moment.

Sofia looked at me with pleasant surprise. If she only knew that I was as surprised as she was. My words were lifting me up as much as they were lifting her. I completely forgot that I'd been crying for help a few days ago. I was speaking as if I knew the way to smile again. Who would have known that I had those words for anyone?

Sofia listened to me intently, as if she was asking me to never stop talking.

We were interrupted when Daisy asked Sofia to come with her outside. They walked away together.

A few minutes later, Sofia came back and talked to me for a while longer. By the end of our conversation, we both felt relieved, refreshed, and hopeful about life. She thanked me. She was going to return to the big city soon, but before she did, she wrote her address on a piece of paper and made me promise to write as often as possible.

And I did. For the next few months we exchanged dozens upon dozens of letters. I found myself experiencing a new kind of joy, a new way of smiling, through each word I wrote to her and each word I read from her in return.

LORENA

The most important thing in my life became writing letters to my new friend, Sofia. The second most important thing was doing well at school. I had to be disciplined not to fail any subject. I would be graduating in about six months.

I had no plans for myself after graduation besides my heart's desire to be joyful, and I knew for that to happen I had to leave my family. The thought of asking Sofia for help had crossed my mind several times after we met, but I didn't dare.

Besides, my family already had a concrete plan for my future after I graduated. Dara had arranged for me to teach at a children's school, made sure I had a husband to marry, and suggested how many children to have, what friends to keep close, and what house to live in.

My heart insisted these plans were not for me. My reality insisted I had no way out. I was stuck in between.

From all the professions my classmates talked about—medical doctor, engineer, and lawyer—being a lawyer sounded good to me. I'd heard all kinds of good stuff about lawyers—that they respected other people, cared about peace, and fought for what was right. Maybe I could do that. In truth, law was just an easy answer to give everyone when they asked about plans after graduation. My real plan was to be joyful!

All the established careers I knew of seemed corrupted in one way or another. Every day I witnessed teachers droning on and on about subjects they had no interest in. Some walked into the classroom without the energy to say hello to any of us. They stood there and threw books at us. It was about killing time and getting their paycheck. Even the few dedicated ones walked around complaining about the low pay. They felt unappreciated by the school system.

I still did well. But the reason I really enjoyed school was Lorena, an introverted girl about my age. We studied in the same class for the last three years of high school. She was also my neighbor, so we got to talk as we walked back home. She was the only classmate I felt comfortable being around.

My tongue didn't sleep much when we were together. It was fun to talk about boys and love. We believed a boy should be our best friend, someone whom we could not only kiss and have fun with, but also someone with whom we could have long conversations about life.

I felt Lorena was more authentic than everybody else. In school, she would get her work done, and was only friendly to those who wanted to be friends with her. She was not a people-pleaser. The world seen through her brown glasses seemed calm and clear. Although she was shy, nothing shadowed her confidence about the things she excelled or believed in.

She wasn't popular at school at all. The other girls tried to make each other envious by wearing outfits like the ones actresses wore on TV. They did this to call attention from the boys. Lorena remained cool. Her white top and tight, funny-looking jeans neither impressed nor changed much during the years we were friends. I admired her and wished I could be more like her. Though I was introverted too, I was always inclined to please others.

While walking back from school one day, we started talking about graduation and what we would do afterward. I'd never talked to her about how I really felt about my family's plans for me. Now was the time.

It began to rain, and we stopped under the awning of a small, bodega grocery store to keep from getting wet. While we waited for the rain to stop, our conversation about graduation day resumed. Lorena asked me about my plans for the hundredth time. She didn't buy into my usual answer about studying to become a lawyer. Somehow, she knew I had other plans.

That day I had something different to say. My joyful plan was more concrete than I'd thought. I took a deep breath. The air was infused with an overpowering aroma of the wetland, lifted by the fresh raindrops. It was not the only overpowering sensation. I also felt an uncontrollable urge to give life to my thoughts through words—thoughts I had been running from, afraid they would be even more dream-like than the lawyer idea. Thoughts to simply be joyful.

Lorena was looking away, watching the rain. I didn't know where to start or how, but I had to do it. We were both quiet for a moment. I guess Lorena was expecting me to remain quiet, or to tell her the lawyer plan again. My fear was that she wouldn't believe me, or wouldn't care.

The stray cat, Aldo, slunk slowly by in the rain. I wished I could become him. He didn't worry about what he needed to do minute by minute; he was content to be Aldo. He didn't care about the drops of rain falling on his body. He seemed to be enjoying every moment of his cat life.

Before Lorena made a move, I took another deep breath and said, "Right after graduation, I am going to move to Salvador to be with my new friend, Sofia."

It felt like these words had been waiting to come from my body for millions of years. It was magical to hear my thoughts becoming something as real as words.

Lorena looked at me, squeezed her eyebrows, tightened her lips, and shook her head. She didn't believe me. I had been exchanging letters with Sofia for months by then, but I'd never talked to her about this. They were my secret joyful plans.

Lorena didn't say anything as she walked away. She didn't need to. I watched her skip and play in the small water puddles the rain left on the ground. I wished the rain would never stop and that I didn't have to go back home. I wanted to become my last words, right then and there.

Desperately, I looked around for Aldo, hoping that if I stared at him hard enough I could still become him before I got home. He was not around. He was simply being Aldo wherever he chose to go.

The silence was too painful. My reality was too real. Thoughts were fun until they became words. Words pressured me to become them.

I walked back home slowly in the light rain. Before I got home, I had already decided to write to Sofia.

YOU CAN COUNT ON ME

That evening, I wrote something along the lines of:

> Dear Sofia,
>
> How is your heart these days? Our last conversation was about hope. Don't forget that we must always believe in our desire to love, and in our desire to end suffering.
>
> Keep moving forward and toward love.
>
> Don't be stuck in hopelessness.
>
> There are so many things to be joyful for, why should we not be so?
>
> I find joy by looking at the top of distant mountains from a tiny crack in my front door. I laugh while balancing a water bucket on my head. I feel calm when I touch a leaf that is close to me while sweating under the hot sun in the plantation field. I get pleasure from listening to music. My fear is gone when I watch everyone eating the food I make.
>
> I know that I believe in love. We must never lose hope.
>
> Speaking of hope, I need to ask you something. When can we speak on the phone?
>
> Com carinho,
>
> Val

She used to call me Val. I didn't really like it, but my name was Valdinelia, and big city people don't have enough time to spend it trying to pronounce such a long name, I assumed. Well, I was really afraid they would like my name, not me. But I was okay with people calling me whatever they wanted, as long as it would please them.

Days later, after sending the letter to Sofia, she wrote me back. She was much more hopeful. The man she was in love with had told her he was going to make a decision soon. He intended to make their relationship official. Her happiness was in every single word I read. I smiled for her!

In the end, she gave me her number and a specific date and time I could call her. I could not hide my smile after that, but I had to; it was still a secret.

As the day approached, I became very anxious. The wait made room for a contradictory conversation in my head. Hope was telling me not to be afraid of what my friend Sofia was going to say when I asked her for help. It told me that no matter what, it would be there with me, right by my side. It even reassured me that I could find another way to leave the town if Sofia said no.

Then there was fear. It insisted that Sofia was going to say no. It said that I must avoid the embarrassment and the pain altogether. I should not speak to Sofia on the phone. Instead, I should write her back and tell her that I didn't have anything to say, that I just wanted to continue to write letters as usual. Fear told me to get real, to accept my fate, and remain where I was.

A third voice joined the conversation. It was my heart. It told me to be calm and trust my feelings of love and joy. They were the only reality that mattered.

I was confused. I was scared to lose hope if Sofia said no. I trusted my heart to remind me of joy and love in case that happened, but without hope, could I listen to my heart? Again, I was caught in-between.

The day came. I got out of bed. Fear said good morning. Hope had breakfast with me. My heart said, "I am here."

I got some money I'd saved. I needed to pay for the operator to make the phone call. It was a long walk. Fear slowed me down with each step I took, while hope tried to push me forward. My heart kept me calm. We had only one tiny booth in town where we could access a phone. The operator was friendly and helpful. I handed her the number on a piece of paper and some coins.

A moment later, the phone rang. When Sofia answered, the woman passed the phone to me.

"Hi, Sofia," I said. All I really wanted to do was speed up our conversation to the end.

"Como vai?" she replied in a cheerful voice.

Hope got closer, as it had promised. Sofia started to talk about her boyfriend, and how happy she was that he seemed finally ready to make a decision about being with her. She thanked me again for keeping her hopeful and calm. She talked for a while and I listened. I was going to need more coins soon.

Then, when I thought we'd need to set up another call for our conversation, she paused and said, "Sorry, I was so excited to tell you the news that I almost forgot you needed to speak to me."

"It's fine; keep talking about the news. We can arrange another phone call," I said with relief. She asked me to talk to her right then. I quickly gave the operator the last coins I had and began. "You know..." I paused to swallow some saliva trapped in my throat. "You know I am graduating soon, right?"

"Yes," she said.

"I don't have a plan, and I don't see myself doing what other people do here," I continued. "They want me to become a school teacher and get married. This is not what I want. So, I'm wondering if you can help me. Can I stay with you for a while? I am a good worker, and I promise to be a loyal friend."

Total silence on both ends. I waited. There was no answer. "Are you there?" I asked after a moment. Fear screamed in my ears, *I told you not to come here. How embarrassing.*

"Are you there, Sofia?" I continued, and this time hope was whispering to me, *She will say yes when you hear her voice again— don't worry.*

We got disconnected for lack of credit. I didn't know if she'd heard me. I ran back home to get some more money to call her again, but the second time, the phone rang and she didn't answer. The operator tried many times for a while. Nothing.

I sat down by the curb in front of the phone booth and wondered if Sofia had heard me. Would she ever talk to me again, now that she knew I needed her help? Why hadn't she answered the phone when I called back? All the answers I got were from fear, but hope was still right with me.

I went home that day and wrote Sofia another letter. I asked if she had heard me on the phone. I told her I had tried calling her back. Then, I asked her again if she could help me.

For each day that passed without an answer from her, fear embraced me tighter and tighter, and hope made me work extra hard.

I focused more on my studies to make sure I passed all my final exams. My heart warmed my thoughts with images of me inside the bus the day after graduation. It was the longest I'd ever had to wait to get a letter back from Sofia.

When I finally got a letter from her, it said, "YES, I heard you on the phone, but got disconnected before I could reply. Then I had to leave quickly to meet my boyfriend. Let's speak on the phone this weekend."

My heart was overflowing with joy. I wanted to tell everyone how happy I was, but unfortunately, my happiness was a secret, too.

Sofia said to call her over the weekend. To me, that meant early Saturday morning. By that time, my conversations with fear and hope were over. It was time for joy to take me to the phone booth!

The phone rang, and Sofia answered in a sleepy voice. "You woke me up. Why so early?"

I looked out at the street and saw lots of people walking around. It was market day.

"I'm sorry. Do you want me to call later?" I asked, hoping she would say no, which she did. She told me that she'd thought about the possibility of helping me for a while, but she was unsure because of the expenses involved. Living in the city was costly. She couldn't guarantee she could find me a job right away.

I promised to look for work on my own, and that I wouldn't let her down in any way. I asked her again to help me. At the end of our conversation, she said she would think about it for a couple of weeks, and then give me a final answer.

Going back home, my heart was still filled with joy like a puppy swinging his tail. Although my body couldn't react with a smile, I knew my life was about to change drastically.

I kept working hard as I prepared to graduate in a few months' time. Weeks went by, and I didn't hear back from Sofia. I called her to find out what was happening. She picked up the phone, but her tears spoke to me before she opened her mouth. Her boyfriend had broken up with her again. He could not commit, she said. She felt lost and didn't know what to do with her life.

"It is a good time for you to come, my friend. I need you close to me," she said.

I felt more motivated to leave town than ever. I had a friend who needed me to ease her pain. I just had no idea how I would tell everyone that I was leaving soon. I also needed money to buy my ticket.

COCONUT CANDY

Graduation day was coming. I would be leaving to stay with Sofia right after. Nobody knew about it, yet, and I had no money.

Studies were going well. I really believed I wouldn't have problems passing the exams. Sofia was waiting for me to tell her the date and time to pick me up at the bus terminal. Money was still an issue, but I was taking care of it.

I would give everyone the news when I was by the door, ready to leave. It was not nice, but I had no other choice. I didn't want to risk being tied to a chair and forced to stay. I didn't know what would happen, so I didn't want to risk it.

As for making some money, Dara had been asking me for a while to sell her homemade *cocadas* (coconut candies) in school. She said I could make good money. A tray filled with the extra sweet treats by the entrance of school would be gone in minutes, she assured me.

I was not convinced, but it was a great time to take her up on her offer. She questioned my "out of the blue" enthusiasm for selling candies at school. There was suspicion in the air, but the idea that she would be making some extra money drove it away.

I was a timid, frightened, and introverted girl. Speaking and writing about love and hope with the only two friends I had, Sofia and Lorena, was what I did best.

It was time to leave my shyness behind for a great cause. On a Monday morning, I left the house holding a tray full of coconut candies. They were covered with a white cloth. It was already hot out, as always. I could feel the heat climbing from my feet to my belly–my sandals were too old to do anything about it. Am I really going to do this? I questioned myself again.

I blushed with shame and fear just thinking about the moment I got in front of other people. I headed to the school's main entrance before the bell rang. It was just a few blocks away.

As I got closer, I heard other children talking, laughing, and giggling. My heart was about to jump out of my mouth. I repeated to myself over and over, *This is just another kind of work I have to do. I need this money to leave town and help my friend Sofia. Go on, do it!*

My thoughts weren't working. I couldn't concentrate on them. Instead, horrifying images of everyone pointing and laughing at me and not buying any *cocadas*, paralyzed me. I paused in the middle of the street and pretended I was fixing my sandals while I listened to fear tell me, *Go back home. Return this embarrassing tray to Dara. Tell her you've changed your mind.*

I had to do it. I needed the money to buy the bus ticket. While I was down pretending to fix my sandals, I saw a line of ants heading to the school entrance. They were carrying something on their backs. They were not ashamed or fearful; they were doing their work. This is what they had to do.

I wish I could become one of these ants, I whispered to myself. I really meant, *I wish I didn't have a mind to think these horrifying thoughts.* I got up and started walking again toward the school. I looked for a shaded place where no one would see me.

I knew there was no point in going there if I were to hide the candies, but I was not one of those ants, yet. Fear was still talking to me.

A boy I'd never seen before came over. He was good-looking, just like a popular actor on TV. What a day to go out there to sell candies! Where did the boy come from?

I quickly tried to hide the tray but it didn't work. He saw it.

"What are you hiding?" he asked with a kind voice.

I couldn't speak; I just looked at him with my fish eyes. Then I stared down at the tray. With shaky hands, I uncovered the candies. I looked back at him, expecting a loud laugh.

The split second in-between, before he reacted, I saw myself running back home in tears. It would be a disastrous end.

To my surprise, his kind eyes seemed to be saying something to me. He gave me a nice smile. I was relieved he was not mean to me. What happened next brought me back to the fear zone.

The boy ran over to the crowded school entrance, stood in front of everyone, and announced, "Look over there." He pointed at me. "Do you see that girl? She has a tray full of delicious candies. Go try one!"

At that moment, I wanted nothing more than an earthquake to split the ground in half. I wanted to be swallowed by a deep, black hole where I couldn't be seen by anyone, myself included.

I closed my eyes for a moment. There was a lot of noise around me. I opened my eyes and saw lots of curious faces looking at the candies. I must have looked pale and cold. I was shaking from head to toe, until I realized that the boy had done me a big favor.

One by one, all the candies were sold in minutes, and I didn't have to do anything but stand there and look strange, mumble the price, and weakly say "thank you" to everyone. Afterward, I looked for the boy with kind fish eyes to thank him. He was not around.

I went back the day after with another tray of candies, and I sold them all again.

That time, on the way, I smiled at the ants carrying their food. I didn't wish to become one of them anymore.

The boy and I met eventually. We sat down after school to talk. He had a long, sad story to tell me about his family. We didn't smile together, but we felt each other's pain. I told him about my plans to leave town. He promised to come visit me in the big city.

Graduation day was close. I hoped my family didn't tie me up on a chair when I told them I was leaving and not coming back.

LEAVING

The big day arrived. I was sixteen-years-old. The bus was leaving at eight o'clock in the morning—hopefully with me inside. I would give everyone the news when I was by the door, ready to leave. It wasn't nice, but I had no other choice. Would they let me leave? I didn't know what would happen, but I didn't want to risk it.

I woke up early and took out my small bag from underneath my bed. It had been packed for days. I carefully folded the last item and placed it inside the bag. It was my high school diploma: a precious asset. It ensured I could get a job to help Sofia pay the bills.

As I reached for the bag to put the paper inside, I saw myself in the mirror. *Is that me?* I asked. I looked so thin. Graduation had been so difficult and stressful that I must have lost more than ten pounds.

I went to the bathroom and then into the kitchen. I had breakfast: bread and butter with coffee and milk. It was still early. Everyone was sleeping.

Back in my room, I pretended I was still asleep. My sister was in a deep sleep. I waited for everyone to wake up so I could tell them I was leaving while they were at the table having breakfast. There was a strange calm in me. It was indifferent to the thoughts that crossed my mind. Fear didn't affect me anymore. Hope embraced me and gratitude filled my heart. There was a feeling of peace and happiness in the moment.

I felt like the man in a story I heard called "The Traveler and The River."

There was a traveler who had been walking in the desert for many, many years. The people he met along the way gave him some water to drink so he wouldn't die. They didn't have much more to give him.

They asked him to join them in their tents and rest for a while. He would always refuse the offers. The man was convinced he would find a flowing river ahead. He kept moving. Everyone told him there was no river to be found and that he would only spend energy in vain and die.

He would simply thank them kindly and move on.

One day, while he was walking, he heard the sound of water droplets. He looked up to see a cloud heavy with water. It started to rain. He stayed there waiting for the rain to stop and fell asleep.

When he woke up, he was by the bank of a flowing river.

I felt like the traveler, as though I was finally resting by the bank of a river that had come to me from above.

Everyone was up. It was time to tell them. I had no ears for fear, no time for doubt, no patience for pain. My heart was guiding me. They were in the kitchen. I stood by the door holding my bag.

Everyone looked at me as if they were seeing a ghost. I told them I was leaving to be with my friend Sofia, who was offering me a place to stay and help in finding a job. There was a moment of total silence as my last words stood there between us.

Then Dara said, "You can't leave like this—all of a sudden. You have a job here and a life that is for you."

I didn't say anything. She didn't seem to oppose my decision, but she had to say something. Jorge never said a word. Ana didn't even know what was happening—Aldo had distracted her. I slowly walked away from the kitchen, crossed the living room, and stepped out the front door.

Walking to the bus station, the same calm and happy feeling I'd felt in my room accompanied me. It was refreshing. Everything in the town looked and felt different. It was as if I was seeing it for the first time, this time with a feeling of renewal mixed with faith!

Inside the bus, a familiar, soothing joy arose in me as I relaxed in one of the seats that had been featured many times in my imagination. I was finally there.

ACARAJÉ

As the bus approached Salvador, hours later, I felt something changing in me. I started to get anxious again. Many thoughts crossed my mind, but one thought dominated them all: My friend Sofia was the only friend or family I had now.

Sofia met me at the bus station. "Sorry, the traffic was horrendous," she said as she kissed me on both cheeks.

To express my gratitude, I gave her a tight hug. My heart was joyful. My mission was to help her feel better and to never regret having helped me leave Bravo.

"You look so much thinner than the last time I saw you," she said.

I didn't say anything. She noticed my thin body, and I felt the sadness in her eyes. She was in pain.

We walked out of the bus station. It was very humid, and I smelled gasoline mixed with *acarajé* patties that were being fried by a lady dressed in a white garment, as if she was going to marry that day.[1]

I stayed close to Sofia, and although the fried smell wasn't pleasant, it got me to acknowledge my hunger. I looked at the fried patties in a bowl as if savoring them with my eyes. Sofia noticed.

"Let's get something to eat, my country friend. You have lost a lot of weight." She laughed.

She was right. I was very hungry, but my weight loss had to do with a different kind of hunger.

We got in her car. Sofia was talking about her second heartbreak, and I was listening. A few minutes later, the air grew heavy with a smell I didn't recognize.

"Look over there. Say hello to Mr. Ocean!" Sofia said.

The smell was coming from the ocean. It was an enormous pool of water—there was no end or beginning. The river I'd once fetched water from was so small in comparison to the ocean. There were waves on the water. People were walking on the sand, and there were some people in the water, too. How could that be possible?

We got out and walked toward a place for something to eat. We sat at a table by the window where I could still see the water. Sofia kept pointing at it. She said I would love walking on the sand

---

1 "Acarajé" is a dish found in West African and Brazilian cuisines and made from peeled beans. These are formed into a ball and then deep fried in dendê (palm oil). Acarajé is traditionally prepared in the northeastern Brazilian state of Bahia, especially in the city of Salvador, where I was. Acarajé is street food, though it also serves as a religious offering to the gods in the Candomblé religion. The dish was brought by slaves from West Africa, and is still cooked in various forms in Nigeria, Ghana, Togo, Benin, Mali, Gambia, and Sierra Leone.

Acarajé consists of cooked and mashed black-eyed peas, seasoned with salt and chopped onions. The beans are molded into a large scone-like patty and deep fried in palm oil in a wok-like pan. The patty is then split in half and stuffed with vatapá and caruru—spicy pastes made from shrimp, ground cashews, palm oil, and other ingredients. There's a vegetarian version served with hot peppers and green tomatoes. Acarajé also comes in a second form called abara, where the ingredients are boiled instead of deep fried.

and swimming in the water. Sofia said she would take me there another day, and that I should learn how to swim. I don't know why, but it didn't excite me. I was excited just to be there.

A man with a stiff walk and a forced smile arrived with a tray. He put a basket of bread and some water on our table. Sofia thanked him and he went away. When we were alone, Sofia began to talk to me about her boyfriend. She cried. She didn't understand why he said that he loved her but couldn't stay with her.

I told her not to give up on his love. I kept listening. For a moment, all I could think about was the bread and butter I was eating. The bread was warm and the butter melting; they were delicious together in my mouth. I didn't understand why Sofia was not enjoying the great-tasting food. There were no problems that could get in the way of my delight in the food. *Isn't Sofia feeling the same?* I wondered, while I watched her sad eyes and listened to her sad words. She was eating too, but the food seemed tasteless to her. *How is that possible?* I asked myself again.

After a while she talked to me about all the great things the city had to offer, including much better restaurants than the one we were eating at. I wondered if better-tasting food would put a smile on her face.

Everything was new, confusing, and uncertain, except Sofia's sadness. When I thought of it, everything became familiar. The unimaginably large town became as small as the palm of my hand. I had a mission that wouldn't let me get lost.

I was there to ease my friend's pain.

SUMMER SOUP

I was all set in the big city. Sofia's apartment was small, but there was enough space for both of us. I felt peaceful in the kitchen making food, or talking to Sofia about life, or cleaning the house. My new home, housework, and life were very different from what I'd had before. It took me a while to stop staring at everything in wonder and awe.

Although it was a large city with many people, I had a strange talent for making complicated things seem and feel very simple, for making large things look small. I didn't know how I learned to do it, but it made me feel safe and comfortable. Having only one or a few people to talk to and trust was enough.

Sofia was the only person who heard me speak. Everyone else she introduced to me needed to guess what my "fish eyes" were trying to say. I heard the neighbor often asking Sofia if I had a tongue. Sofia always laughed and replied that my tongue was only awake when she was around.

I needed to find a job soon to help Sofia pay the bills. But I also had to help her to feel better when she was sad, or if she needed me for anything. This was my life—the size of the town didn't matter.

In less than a month, my routine changed. Sofia got me a job interview with one of her doctor friends whose receptionist had moved back to her small town.

I met the doctor, who seemed nice and cool. When I introduced myself to him, he said right away that he didn't like my name; well I didn't either. I could tell we would be friends.

He called me Val. Everyone there called me Val, in fact. I didn't really mind. I'd never felt I belonged to a name, or that a name belonged to me. The sound of my name scared me. Every time Dara had screamed my name I knew something hurtful would come next.

I remembered clearly the day I was playing with other kids around a fence that was made of sharp metal. Dara called me, and I responded to her voice so quickly that I didn't see the fence in front of me. I threw myself into it and tangled my body in the fence. A piece of sharp metal cut my cheek so badly the fragment could be seen from the inside of my mouth. I thought I would die that day.

So, the doctor and I were friends already. The money wasn't much, but I would still be able to help Sofia with rent. This meant a lot to me. I was very grateful for what she had done. I started working at the office. The job was about ten hours a day.

The work was hard and seemed complicated in the beginning, but soon I did everything well—so well that the doctor kept saying he had never made as much money as he did with me. I worked hard for him, then cooked dinner every night for Sofia.

Her favorite dish was soup! After I cleaned everything, we talked about love and hope. I made sure to be around for my friend to support her as often as I possibly could.

Sofia was still quite sad. She couldn't stop sobbing. Her boyfriend couldn't commit. I was there for her in person as I had been through the letters. My heart was grateful for my new life, but I would have liked to have been more joyful and to have worked less.

My new job started to become heavier and heavier. At least once a week, the doctor's wife would show up to deliver a strange kind of performance. In the waiting room, packed with patients, she threw temper tantrums.

She was a pretty, young, well-educated lady. She had a successful career in business and dressed in a formal, expensive white suit. But when she opened her mouth, she sounded like one of the ladies out on the street by the bus stop—the ones who begged for pennies and then got mad when someone didn't give them anything.

She called me names aloud and demanded I tell her about her husband's whereabouts, as if I knew. She believed I was working for him not as a receptionist, but as an agent for his extramarital affairs. Her words were filled with anger and frustration. They were meant to hurt me, and they did. Her husband was a laidback, overweight man who seemed clueless about her behavior.

I was caught between her stormy words and the doctor's indifference. When she made a scene, he calmly came to Reception, put his arms around her, and walked her out of the room. She would give me one last angry look before going away. I hadn't done anything to deserve it. I worked hard for her husband to make extra money by scheduling a large number of clients. They kept me there late. There was so much she didn't know about me. I liked to make everything simple and small, and her behavior seemed way too complicated and big for me.

A typical day at the office consisted of non-stop, stressful work answering the phone, which rang by the second. I acted like I was the happiest person on Earth in front of patients. There was no time to give any genuine attention to anyone, but I did my best.

But when the doctor's wife came to deliver her angry performance, I finished the day even more exhausted than usual. On those days, the scalding summer evening couldn't warm up my heart. I needed an extra hot bowl of soup and a soulful conversation with Sofia. We normally ended the day this way, anyhow.

CARNIVAL AND GRILLED CHEESE

I had been in Salvador for over two months. The Carnival was starting soon. Coming home from work, I already could see the city changing. It began to look like the street market back in my small town, early in the morning. The vendors were setting up their tents to showcase their produce. Everyone told me the Carnival in Salvador, Bahia, was one of largest street parties on Earth.

Sofia didn't really like it. She said it was too crowded, confusing, and violent. She usually left the city during this time for somewhere quieter, but she decided to stay this year to take me to the streets. It was my first time and she was excited for me.

The Carnival began. It was all over the news on TV, but I still didn't know what to expect. It was a scalding Saturday afternoon. We put on shorts, tank tops, and sneakers. I was so glad Sofia was my size. I wore her clothes and shoes all the time. All the money I made I handed to her. I never had a penny to buy anything. So if I needed anything besides food, I needed to ask her. If I was sick, Sofia's mother took care of me. They were my family now.

We walked to the bus stop by our building and took the bus to the main area where the party had started. On the bus, there were lots of people wearing the same kind of colorful T-shirts with a name written on them. I asked Sofia why they were dressed that way.

She said they were members of a "bloco"—a group of people who are fans of a specific band that plays in Carnival. These bands play on top of enormous, fancy trucks, and people in the bloco follow the truck around the city, singing and dancing.

Blocos were separated from the general public on the street by a thick rope that went around the truck. The rope was held in place by poor people hired by the organizers of the bloco. Anyone could participate in these blocos, but to do so they needed to pay a lot of money. Some people paid installments all year round to be part of these groups.

I understood what Sofia was saying. These people inside the blocos were "special."

We got off the bus. There were people in every direction, only a few inches away from me—breathing on my neck, pushing me out of their way. Most of them were not wearing the colorful T-shirts. They were in normal clothes like Sofia and me. Others were selling food, water, candies, ice cream, and of course, lots of alcohol.

We walked toward the ocean. The music was loud. We were squeezed and pushed all the way to the beach. People passed by us going in all directions. We found an open area close to the ocean on top of a hill.

Sofia told me it was a good place to stay. We could wait there for the next band to pass by in its enormous, fancy truck followed by the colorful T-shirt people. The view was incredible on top of the hill. I watched the waves in the water and the people walking on narrow streets on the opposite side. They looked like the lines of ants I used to watch in my small town, except they were not carrying food on their backs, but rather cups or bottles of alcohol in their hands. I didn't want to be that kind of ant.

While we were sitting on the grass, a child came by selling grilled cheese. He must have been about ten-years-old. I wondered where his parents were. He called us "auntie" and said that one cheese stick cost only two reais. His eyes were fixed on our pockets. To him we were not humans, but pockets with money.

I asked Sofia what a child was doing in a place like this where anyone could get lost easily. Wasn't it dangerous? Sofia asked the child about his parents. He pointed somewhere far from us where there were hundreds of people walking around. We doubted his parents were anywhere near.

He insisted we buy the cheese. Sofia didn't do it. Instead, she asked him, "What will you do with the money, little boy?"

He said he would give it to his mother. She would then buy him and his sisters food. He said that while looking down and playing with his dirty fingers.

Sofia gave him two reais and asked him to eat the cheese when he got hungry. He tucked the money inside his worn-out sneakers, smiled at us, and walked away. For a brief moment, I reflected on what life was all about as I watched the boy disappear into the crowd.

The band on top of the truck passed by a few minutes later. The music excited me. It was so loud. I couldn't stop my body from moving, so I started to dance. My heart was beating with the drums. Sofia was dancing a little too, but she looked distracted and sad at times. She didn't seem to be having as much fun as I was. Her boyfriend's station was on in her head, playing a louder song.

We followed the truck for a while, stopping only to drink some water. I managed to transform this extremely crowded and confusing situation into a small and simple one. My heart was safe with Sofia at my side; she reminded me what my life was about. Being there with her reminded me of my mission to help her feel hopeful about love.

The truck was reaching the end of its path. As we stopped to get some water, a young man approached Sofia. They moved off to a quieter area and started to talk. I was left looking at the people passing by, wondering how long I would be there alone.

Sofia came back smiling minutes later, waving a piece of napkin. Written on it was the number of the man she'd been talking to.

She was very excited. She said they had arranged to go to the beach together the next day. He liked quieter places more than the crowded streets that time of year. They had a lot of things in common. She seemed to be forgetting her boyfriend already. It was a good thing, I guessed. Both of us headed home that day with tired bodies but happy minds, for different reasons.

THERE WAS MUSIC, NEVERTHELESS

The next day, the phone rang before noon. It was Sofia's Carnival guy. She said he was coming to pick her up so they could spend the day together. She was very excited.

Soon after the phone call, Sofia said goodbye and left.

She came home a week later to pick up some of her clothes. She seemed to have found a new love. She told me she would be staying with him for a few more days. We hugged each other and said goodbye. I had no idea that my life was about to change again. From then on, when I came home from work, Sofia was never there. She didn't pick up the phone when I called either. Little by little, the apartment started to look like one of those home furnishing stores after a clearance sale. There was less and less furniture every day. I had no idea what was happening. Sofia never said a word to me. But I wasn't panicking. Sofia wouldn't disappear like that. I was positive she would either come back or take me with her.

It didn't happen.

After a few weeks, I had only a mattress and some kitchen utensils left. The neighbor came to give the news that I had to leave the apartment in two weeks. It would be rented to someone else. I didn't know what to do. I had a little money put away, but not much, since I had been giving most of it to Sophia. Being in the city and in that apartment without Sofia was like switching from color TV to black and white. I sobbed and sobbed every night.

A week before I had to leave the place, Sofia's new boyfriend showed up and handed me a small radio. She knew how much I enjoyed listening to music and dancing. He also gave me a newspaper opened to the section 'Rooms for Rent.'

I asked him about Sofia. He said she was happy and she wished me good luck.

After he left, I sat down on the floor. My tears wouldn't stop falling. Why would she leave like that? It didn't make any sense.

I could hear the ocean waves at night, and had the strange feeling that they could hear me, too. *Isn't there enough salty liquid around here?* I asked myself. *Why does this place need mine?*

I felt sad, anxious, and lost. I didn't know what would happen next. I had no friends or family to help me in the city. This was a big, complicated problem I had no idea how to make simple and small. I thought about my parents, but going back to their house was not an option.

CRAWLING FORWARD

My best friend, Sofia, was gone, and I had very little money and no home to go back to.

After a tough night trying to sleep, I woke up and called some ads offering a room for rent. I had no time or extra money to pay bus fare to visit a place. I had to agree to rent one over the phone. When the day came to move, I packed the same small bag—which was now only a bit fatter than when I'd left my small town.

I took the bus to my new home. It was a long ride, but I knew where to get off. When I got off, the streets were empty. It was late in the day on a weekend. I saw a boy selling grilled cheese on a stick crossing the street in front of me. He reminded me of the Carnival day with Sofia.

I walked in the direction of the house, but I wished I was lost. The further I went, the narrower, dirtier, and scarier the streets became, and the older the houses.

Near the place, there was an old homeless man in front of an abandoned house I passed. I could see only his eyes. His clothes and the cracked walls of the house were almost the same color. I knocked on the door of my new home and waited. The homeless man was staring at me.

Minutes later, an obese lady answered the door. She didn't make eye contact, and I could hardly understand her when she spoke. She was out of breath. I told her my name. She asked me to come in.

The place was old, dark, and smelled like burnt food. I walked behind her through a long, narrow corridor. She showed me the house and my room. I laid my bag on the bed while she waited by the door. I paid her and started unpacking. It didn't take very long. I put the radio on a low volume.

There were a few pieces of furniture in the room: a bed, a nightstand, a dresser, and a small rug on the floor. Everything was very old; the room needed more light. When I was about to leave to go to the kitchen, a young guy poked his head in the door and said hi to me. He had a calm, shy smile on his face.

"My name is Zé," he said.

I introduced myself as Val, and we walked toward the kitchen. Zé was friendly. He looked older than me, but not by much. He was shy and had large, curious green eyes. He didn't talk much but stared at me a lot.

The smell of burnt food was stronger in the kitchen. Zé stood close to me while I found space in the cabinet to put away some cups and a bag of crackers I'd brought. Then we sat down on the sofa in the living room.

Zé and I talked about how we'd found the place, and shared a bit about our life stories. I only talked about the positive things, and he did the same. I guess we wanted to keep our conversation light. He asked me if I was hungry and walked away. A few minutes later, he came back with a plate of fried patties made of eggs and vegetables. He said he'd made them earlier, and that they were very tasty.

I didn't know why, but I had a feeling I shouldn't be eating his food, although it did look good and I was very hungry. I took one patty, thanked him, and let him know that I was very tired. I needed to go to my room and sleep.

We said good night and went in opposite directions. My room was up front, close to the entrance of the house, while his was in the back somewhere.

The night was scalding hot. I wore a long, light shirt. I didn't want to use the bedsheet to cover my body. I lay down and fell asleep.

Perhaps a few hours passed. I woke up with a tickling sensation on my legs and back, going up to my neck. It was very dark, and I couldn't see anything. But I felt like there were insects all over me. I didn't want to believe my thoughts.

I reached down to feel my leg and touched a big, crawling insect. I got up at once, desperately looking for the light switch, shaking my body to throw off the bugs. I tried not to scream, but inevitably I did. When the light was on, I saw that the bed was infested with huge cockroaches. Some were still crawling on the bed, but most had fled to the walls around the room.

I opened the door and stood in the corridor, hoping somebody had heard me scream. I waited there for a while, but no one came.

I was used to nightmares, but I didn't know what to do about this real one.

There was no way I could go back to that bed and sleep again. I found my way to the living room, feeling along the walls, and tried to sleep on the sofa. Hours went by. Sitting in the dark room, I knew there was one thing I couldn't do anymore, and that was cry. I stayed up for a while, lost in fear, hoping the sun would rise soon. I woke up with the big lady shaking me by the shoulder.

"Why are you here?" she asked. Part of me knew this was a question I should answer, but another part of me hoped it was just a dream I didn't have to respond to. I could hardly think. She insisted.

My head was spinning. I found a way to tell her what happened. She laughed and walked away. Her reaction was strange, but to me it was just another sad thing to add to the pile of sadness that was my life at that time.

Minutes later, she came back with a spray bottle. She instructed me to spray that liquid all over the room before I went to bed every night. I could only thank her. The liquid smelled awful. I wasn't sure who would be more uncomfortable: the roaches or me. Either way, my nights there wouldn't be restful. It meant I needed to look for a new place at the end of the month.

Coincidence or not, when I got to work on Monday morning, I was fired. The doctor said he couldn't have me there anymore. His wife wouldn't let him.

I didn't understand. I thought we'd had a great business relationship. He was making more money with me than he'd made with any other secretary. There was no strength left in me to fight for my job.

He paid me for a month's work, gave me a little extra, and wished me good luck. I kept my promise: no crying. I must move forward. There was enough salty water out there—I wouldn't add to it. I held the tears hostage in my body. They were used to it.

IT'S 9AM

Coming back from the doctor's office on the bus, I started thinking that before I ran out of money, I must find another job. I got off the bus and walked in the opposite direction from my place. I wanted to see what the other side of the neighborhood was like.

In Brazil, neighborhoods are designed the same way: One side is very poor and falling apart, and the other is rich and prosperous. One is next to the other. A few people from the poor area rebel and become criminals, but the majority conform and become servants of the rich.

The rich have a love/hate relationship with the poor; they are forced to build fortresses around their houses, install fancy security systems in their businesses, and buy bulletproof cars. They are forced to have the poor in their houses and businesses working hard for very little.

I saw a very nice square with fancy stores, lots of new cars, and big houses with gardens. I walked for a while, not sure what to look at or for. I stopped to buy a warm corn on the cob to eat. Standing there, I realized I was in front of a drugstore. There was a sign in the window looking for a receptionist. I couldn't believe it.

I went in and asked if I could apply. A woman gave me a form to fill out. My heart filled with hope as I gave the completed form back to her. She said the boss would call me if he was interested.

I walked back home with different thoughts than I'd had earlier on the bus. I felt as though my life would get better soon—but not soon enough, as it turned out. When I got home, I discovered Zé had been in my room. He had left a lipstick wrapped in gift paper and some food for me on the top of the dresser. A few minutes later, he came in with his big, shy smile, asking if I liked the gifts. He seemed to be waiting for me to come home, like a husband waits for his wife. I was very uncomfortable at this point; I didn't want to be rude when he was so friendly, but I had to put an end to this. He was going too far.

I screamed at him to get out of my room immediately. The words came out of me in an angry burst. I felt bad for Zé. Watching him leave without a smile hurt me more than it hurt him, but I had to do it.

He left my room, and from that day on I started closing and locking my door more often. It was horrible because I was trapped with the heat and roach poison spray inside. There were no windows. I needed to make a tough choice every night, between a hot, dark room with roaches all over me and the smell of poison in the air or Ze trying to sneak into my room with gifts and food.

Days after I filled out the application form for the secretary position at the drugstore, the phone rang. The only phone I had was the landline of the house I lived in. The big lady, who still laughed when she looked at me, came to the room to announce someone was looking for me.

I rushed out, squeezing my body between the lady and the wall of the narrow corridor to answer the phone.

"Good morning," I said, trying to sound as polite as I could.

"Good morning, is this Val-di-ne... ?" He struggled to pronounce my long name.

I helped him with the pronunciation and asked him to call me Val. He was brief and his voice sounded harsh. For a moment, I thought he was scolding me for something, or maybe he was taking a break from a fight with someone else.

I was extra kind with my voice and words. The job would be good for me. It was close to home. I could walk there and not spend money on bus fare. The man from the drugstore said he would like to see me for an interview that afternoon.

We hung up the phone, and I got ready to go over there. I took a shower and wore the blue dress uniform from my previous job with the doctor. It didn't take long to get there.

There was a young woman wearing a large necklace with a cross at the desk up front. She asked me to take a seat and wait to be called to the owner's office. The man who I would be working for, if I was hired, owned the place. A moment later, the woman told me I could go in to see the boss.

The door was unlocked. I walked in and closed it behind me. The man was on the phone. He took a quick look at me, favoring other parts of my body besides my face, and went back to his conversation. The office was a small room filled with papers and medicine boxes. The man's table took up most of the space. I squeezed in and took a seat in one of the chairs in front of his table. There were a few opened boxes of medicine and a glass of water on the table.

He hung up the phone, stood, and went straight to the coffee machine without saying a word to me. He came back with a cup of coffee and gave me a strange look. I didn't say anything.

The conversation now was between him and his coffee. He held the cup up close to his mouth and nose, smelled it, and sipped it for a while without saying anything to me. I stayed quiet too, and watched him enjoy his coffee moment.

He put the cup down on the table between his pills and the newspaper, looked at me, and said in a loud voice, "You are hired. Come and start tomorrow at seven a.m., and don't be a second late!" He shouted the last words extra loudly, as if I were already outside his office, perhaps even on the street. I thanked him and left. The interview had not actually been an interview, and he never said anything about paying me, but I needed the job.

The next day, I woke up extra early so I wouldn't be a second late. I got there at six-thirty a.m. There was an older man working at the drugstore. I said hello to him and introduced myself. Everyone working there was so anxious, but they seemed to try hard to look calm and cold, which made them look strange.

I walked to the desk where the woman had been sitting yesterday. I guessed it was my desk now. I sat there and waited for someone to come and tell me what to do. Nobody did.

At eight o'clock, I heard someone ask, "Did she come at seven?"

I couldn't hear the other person's answer. Instead, I heard loud footsteps coming toward the desk. It was my new boss. He passed by me so quickly I couldn't even see his face. He was saying so many things as he walked by that I couldn't understand anything.

"Why didn't you make me coffee?" he shouted as he came back toward me. Before I could say anything to him, he asked me to look for someone who could teach me to make coffee.

My whole first day at the new job I was scolded for not doing things I didn't know I was supposed to do, and for not doing things correctly. However, I knew that learning new tasks and working hard were things I could do well. If I could learn the job fast enough, I would be safe.

Under a thunderstorm of angry shouts and verbal insults, I learned everything that could be learned at that place, maybe more. I took all the calls on the first ring, I organized the boss's schedule, hosted his visitors, made him fresh coffee in the morning and afternoon, brought him lunch, and cleaned and organized his office. I was never late, and I did everything my boss asked me to do, including getting under his desk to remove his shoes before I served him coffee. He said it was part of my job. I worked from seven in the morning until late at night, since I could only leave after he left. Pretty often, he left close to nine at night.

Walking home late at night was another scary part of the day. I needed to walk fast and look tough, which I didn't think convinced anyone. There were drunks, drug addicts, and prostitutes on the way home. I felt their eyes following me. It was just like being in one of my nightmares. I pretended I didn't see the scary images and kept moving, trying not to show my fear. I forced myself to imagine that I was bigger than they were and that I scared them instead. It didn't work.

My boss was often one of those scary images, but when I looked at him and he gave me his strange, calm smile, it made all my work worthwhile. Sometimes though, I felt as though I was around Dara. I could have tried finding another job where my boss wouldn't scream at me or treat me the way he did, but I felt committed to him. He felt like a child who needed care.

I had been locking the door so Zé couldn't come in at night, which made it hard to sleep. One day, I couldn't get to sleep until dawn. The heat was too intense with the door locked, and the smell was unbearable. I must have used too much of the roach poison spray. I overslept and woke up around nine o'clock when the lady started knocking heavily on my door. I couldn't tell if I was asleep or awake. I didn't know how she could recognize me as a person; I certainly didn't feel at all like myself. The lady told me my boss had been calling by the minute looking for me. She told me what time it was. Only then did I realize I was very late for work.

Fear took over me. I rushed into the bathroom and collapsed onto the floor. My stomach hurt so much I couldn't move, and my body shook uncontrollably. I felt weak. My thoughts were confusing. Moment by moment I feared I would get beaten, then that I would get fired, then I feared the roaches, Zé, and not having a place to live or money. All these thoughts paralyzed me. I couldn't move from the floor.

The lady knocked on the door, telling me to get out of there and talk to my boss on the phone. He was waiting. I wanted to find a way to vanish before I had to walk through that door. Soon after her knocking stopped, I got up from the floor, opened the door, and walked toward the phone. My heart was racing. I didn't think I could speak.

As soon as he knew I was on the other end, he screamed as loud as he could, "You are fired! Never come around my drugstore. I don't want to see you ever again."

I spent the day in my room, not sure what to do next. I felt like an elderly woman whose body couldn't move anymore. I was stuck. I couldn't stay, and I couldn't leave. Later that evening, without shedding any tears, I turned inward: *What can save me?* I had a dream that became a revelation.

Chapter 3

From Pain to Fitness

The next day I woke up and remembered the vivid dream I'd had. I was standing on a platform. There were a few people nearby. A man got very close to me and whispered in my ear that he loved me. I felt embraced by the warmth of his words. He was right by my side. I felt safe. The man repeated that he loved me over and over. He had an accent and I couldn't see his face. The imagery of the dream was not clear, but it impressed me with a clarity that went beyond a dream.

I woke up grateful for having the dream. The feeling of warmth from knowing someone loved and cared about me was so real. There was nothing in my reality that resembled that feeling. My heart was filled with an unexplainable joy, and my hope was renewed.

It was the weekday. Instead of looking for a new job, I decided to do something else. I would go to the biggest mall in the city that afternoon and have the largest size chocolate mousse from the best deli there. Chocolate mousse was my favorite dessert.

After breakfast, I spent the whole morning beautifying myself. I washed my hair, soaked it with leave-in conditioner to tame the curls, and tried on a few outfits. I didn't have many options, but I wanted to look my best. I found an outfit Sofia gave me as a gift—a long black skirt that went with a silky, golden top I'd never worn before. Walking to the bus stop, the eyes upon me and the scary streets I had to navigate didn't scare me anymore. I was safe in the warmth of my heart, accompanied by the memories of my dream. I could feel the man's love. Plus, there was a large cup of chocolate mousse waiting for me.

People looked at me as I got on the bus. I might have been a bit overdressed for the bus at that time of day, but I knew my clothes reflected the feelings in my heart; they were clean and new. I took an empty seat by the window. It wasn't that I liked the view of the city much, but I liked riding the bus because I felt like I was moving forward in my life. It made me believe life could still take me somewhere I wished to be, if I only followed the heart, feelings which told me to celebrate life with joy anywhere and at any time.

I got off the bus at the mall and took the escalator to the third floor where the food court was. It was crowded and noisy. People were looking at shop display windows, wishing they could have those things. For a moment, I had the impression I was living a different reality than the one they were living. My window view was from my heart. It showed me simple ways to be joyful, like riding the bus or eating chocolate mousse.

But the dream I'd had last night had created a desire in me. I would like to be with a man who could love me that way. I sighed.

There was a long line at the dessert place. The smell was overwhelmingly delicious. My eyes were fixed on the large chocolate mousse displayed in the window. I was just like those people downstairs staring at windows.

Soon, there was just one person in front of me. Moments later, I was walking from the dessert stand holding my large chocolate mousse and a plastic spoon, looking for an empty table where I could sit and have my dessert. I saw an empty table almost hidden in a far corner. It was the perfect one, since I was very shy.

I rushed to grab the cozy table, but before I got there, my spoon fell.

Before I could go back to get another one, someone appeared in front of me and said, "Oi," ("Hi" in Portuguese) with an accent. "I will help you get a clean spoon," he continued.

My trip to the mall is ruined, I thought. There was a man in the way of my cozy chocolate mousse moment. It was the only reason

I was in the crowded and noisy mall. I couldn't believe it. In that moment, I didn't connect the man with my dream. I had chocolate on my mind.

Although he spoke with an accent, he looked Brazilian. His tan skin was very much like mine; his hair was black, too. He was almost my height, which is to say, short.

His name was Edward.

AN EARLY MARRIAGE: I DREAMT OF LOVE

Moments after we met, I realized it was something of a coincidence with the dream I had. But the man didn't make me feel the way the dream had. I didn't like people who didn't speak my language well. I felt we wouldn't be able to understand each other. Clear communication was very important to me. Sofia's cousins used to date foreigners, and every time they tried to hook me up with one of them, I would cross my arms and refuse to speak a word.

So there I was with one of those people who I thought couldn't speak my language. It surprised me greatly that he could actually communicate very well in Portuguese. His voice sounded a bit funny, but I could understand him.

He walked with me back to the dessert place and got me a new spoon. He was very energetic and talkative. I was starting to like him. Although he seemed anxious, I sensed his kind heart.

We found a table in the middle of the crowded food court and sat down. He was an American, a history teacher who had been living and working for a private school in Salvador for almost a year now. He loved the arts, read classic novels, and listened to classical music. We spent hours together at that table. He talked to me about his country (especially New York, where he'd lived for a year), and the time he spent in Europe; he loved the wine, the food, the different languages, and the architecture. He also talked about Salvador; he was fascinated with the culture, didn't like the food much, and also thought the system was cruel and corrupt. He said he taught kids who didn't know anything about the poor neighborhood next door to their school, and how the rich lived in a bubble there, accumulating wealth while pretending all the poverty around them didn't exist. It all intrigued and entertained me, but I really wanted to know more about him.

After a while, Edward started talking about what hurt him. How unfair other people and life had been to him. He said he was a great man with a big heart who only wanted to help others, but never made the money he deserved. He had my total attention. I asked him to tell me more while I ate my chocolate and listened to his story. At one point, he almost cried.

The hours went by fast, till at last it was night. Edward said he needed to go and offered to take me home. I told him that I could go home alone, that the bus took me to my door. This was not true, but I was hesitant to get in a car with him. Edward said he would take the bus with me to make sure I got home safe.

When he said that, memories of the dream appeared in my mind. Could he be the man of my dream? I'd never met anyone who cared about my safety. My heart was filled with joy.

Sitting beside him on the bus, I thought of nothing but how kind Edward was being to me. He was still talking about his sad past, but I heard only the beautiful, warmhearted words coming from him.

I didn't feel time passing during the short ride. As he was walking me home from the bus stop, I noticed he was getting closer and closer to me. I wasn't sure if he was trying to embrace me in a romantic way, or if he was trying to protect himself or me from the scary streets and people around us. Edward was clearly horrified by the neighborhood I lived in.

"I can't believe this is where you come and go every day," he said in awe. Until that moment, he had only talked about himself. Now he started to ask a lot more questions about me. How long had I lived there, did I live with my family, where was my family, what happened to me to be in a place like that, who were the people in the house, and many other questions. I told him part of my story. He was extremely horrified even with the short version of my life story. Edward made me feel as though I now had someone in the world who cared about me.

He called a cab. Before he went back outside to wait for it, he asked me for a piece of paper and a pen. He wrote his number and took mine. Edward said he would call me soon. As the taxi took him away from me, I wished I was inside that car.

YOU ARE BLOCKING MY VIEW

Between the heat and the smell of roach poison, it was hard to fall asleep. Yet I had a magical and intense feeling about Edward that neutralized any physical discomfort. I wished the night was over so I could meet Edward again. He was my new sun.

I woke up tired. Thoughts of him welcomed me to a new day, but it really felt like a welcome to a new life.

I found a job at a nearby textile store. My first day on the job, they gave me a uniform. It was an orange T-shirt and some black pants. No dresses there, which made me happy. I didn't need to look cute wearing a dress to do my job. All I needed to do was cut the fabric straight and be polite to customers. On my first day, I noticed that everyone who worked at the store was happy. It was such a different environment from the doctor's office and the drugstore, not to mention my family's house and Sofia's apartment. My own place, with Zé staring at me, the heat, and the roach poison, had become happy, too. It didn't occur to me that happiness was never out there but within one's own heart, and that a happy heart can create a happy reality all around us. A few days later, Edward called me. He wanted to take me out that weekend.

In the cab that Saturday, he asked about my week and apologized for not calling me earlier. The car stopped by the ocean, and we walked on the sidewalk near the water. It was a mild evening. I couldn't remember the last time I'd felt so good. The fresh breeze alone made it a beautiful experience. I felt safe.

As we walked to an Italian restaurant, Edward talked about his week at school and how unsatisfied he was with the students, the parents, and the administrators. He complained for quite a while. I didn't know what to say to him. He picked a table by the window overlooking the ocean. It was a beautiful, serene view, but I'd have rather seen a beautiful and serene Edward.

Edward placed the order for both of us. I had no idea what I was going to eat, but I liked that he had so much experience with these things. I didn't drink alcohol, but I tried to be polite and sip from the glass he ordered for me.

The wine tasted awful. I coughed with every sip. He laughed, although it wasn't funny. I was drinking it to please him and to see him smile. We talked about many things. Talking was tastier than the food to me. I'd finally met a man who talked to me about life, and listened to what I had to say, too. Edward looked at me attentively when I talked about love, how it was the foundation for a joyful life. He would agree, but then right after he would say that education and money were the foundation of a good life. He was a bit too insistent about it. I felt he was trying to convince me of something. We were in a polite, intentional tug-of-war.

While we were eating and talking, two young children pressed their faces and hands against the window close to us. They looked down at our plates.

"These are homeless children. They are all over the city," I told Edward.

He said he already knew about them, and that they annoyed him by asking for money all the time—on the street, at the beaches, in front of his building, everywhere. Edward seemed irritated. He called the waiter to chase the children away. He said they were spoiling his dinner and blocking his view.

I felt lucky to be on the other side of that window, yet I felt the window wasn't the only thing separating happiness from unhappiness; Edward's mentality was, too.

For a moment, I questioned my perception of him as a kind man. He seemed to only be kind to me. I needed that, especially at that moment, but someone who is truly kind expands his love to everyone.

We finished eating and he paid the bill, which was probably close to my room's monthly rent. I thanked him. As we went for a walk on the sand by the ocean, he began to talk about love in a different way. He said he was almost forty years old, but never married because he believed in real love. Edward was twenty years older than me, although he looked much younger than his age, and I felt much older than him.

"To truly love someone is to surrender. It's to give yourself to the other completely," he said, looking at the ocean.

I asked him, "Why do you think you haven't given yourself to another in all these years?"

"I never found a woman who was worthy of my love to the point of committing for life," he said, this time looking at me.

"What makes a woman worthy of your love, Edward?"

"A woman who understands the real me."

"Are you being the real you now, with me?"

"Yes, I am always the real me. But other people don't seem to see me for who I really am." Edward looked at me, as if wishing I could be the one to see the real him.

"What do you mean by people not seeing you for who you are?"

He said, "I am not seen as loving and kind all the time, but I have a good heart and good intentions."

"Shouldn't love, kindness, and good intentions be visible through one's words and actions?"

He was quiet for a while, then changed the subject.

We kept walking on the beach under the moonlight. I already had the feeling that I knew Edward better than he knew himself.

He took me to his home to show me pictures. It was a pleasant evening. After calling a cab for me, he kissed me on the lips and told me to prepare my heart—he had lots of surprises coming for me.

LOVE OR A MISTAKE?

In the days after our first date, my thoughts, actions, and words were dedicated to Edward. He was the center of my life. Nothing bothered me as much anymore—the dark house I lived in, the roaches in my room, Zé, or the absence of my friend, Sofia—not even the staring eyes upon me as I walked back and forth from my job on the streets. I looked forward to seeing Edward again for our long tug-of-war conversations about love and money, the delicious food we ate, and his smile while I made faces sipping wine.

We started seeing each other more often, and within a month, I felt I knew all the best places and restaurants in town. Edward's conversations had changed a bit, too. Before, he talked a lot about his exciting life experiences; now, he wanted me to experience what he did. He'd say that he hoped the investment would be worth it for both of us.

I was not sure what the word "investment" meant to him. I thought it was a translation problem. His Portuguese was good, but not great. The more comfortable I got around Edward, the more I talked to him about love. He often laughed and said I was too romantic.

Edward started to change my life in ways I never imagined. I had no idea what money could do until I met him. In less than two months, it felt like I had been born again. It was like my entire past was gone.

He asked me to quit my job and to move to a place close to his apartment. He lived in one of the most expensive neighborhoods in Salvador. It was a few blocks from the beach. He told me not to worry about money. He would take care of everything, so that I could focus on my potential. He sounded really serious about it, but to me it simply felt good.

I moved into a private room at a penthouse, a sphere-shaped high-rise building with an incredible ocean view. Although I didn't enjoy going to the beach, waking up with the ocean staring at me first thing in the morning was beyond my dreams.

The older widow who owned the place rented the rooms, many of which were home to students. She was a mother figure to all of us. She cooked, and at meal times she would talk to us about the importance of healthy foods and exercise.

She worked out every day and read books, but I never saw her smile. All the beauty and luxury of her apartment, even its incredible panoramic ocean view, couldn't put a smile on her face. In some ways, though, I understood her, since I'd had the opposite experience—I had known joy among poverty and chaos. Now all the material comfort was starting to grow on me. While my earlier joy had been filled with serenity, this was a new happiness that came with excitement.

My life had quickly turned into something I'd never imagined. I was taking English lessons in the morning, and going to dance lessons after—ballet and Flamenco. Then I had lunch, computer class, and then went to the gym later in the afternoon. Everything was within walking distance.

Edward took me to the hair salon every week. My curly hair was straightened and turned almost blonde. I did my nails and wore makeup, too. My whole wardrobe changed. Even my name changed: Edward called me Valeria. He said it was close to "Valerie" in English. I was now reading novels. I did my best with everything so I could impress Edward and show my gratitude for what he was doing for me.

Everything was new and exciting to me, but nothing was more interesting than exercise. He had introduced me to exercise and eating healthily. I didn't look up to the sky anymore or touch the trees and plants around me; everything was replaced by the mirror. My physical image was becoming the new way to feel good. Admiring the way I looked helped to release the pain still trapped in my body through the memories of my early past. Before I became a fitness enthusiast, my body weight was controlled by my emotional condition. I pleased those around me regardless of the way they treated me. I needed to be loved and accepted by others to feel good about myself. I was never fat, but would gain weight as quickly as I would lose it. It all depended on how others made me feel through their behaviors. Exercising and eating quality foods improved my general health, stabilizing the up-and-down weight problem.

I was turning twenty when I met my first husband. I married him and, simultaneously, my addiction to exercise began. I saw how much the result of my working out and dieting pleased him, but it never ended: My need for his compliments and praise redoubled. It didn't take long to realize that working on my body earned me extra "certificates of self-worth" not only from my husband, but from everybody else I met, both inside and outside of the gym. I had found a "fountain of love," but it was the kind of fountain I couldn't bathe in without someone else's help. All I needed to do was keep working on my body and be in great shape all the time.

This is how my addiction with exercise and dieting began. I had no idea how much my mind dwelled in the past and on the future, or how I was creating such a negative present. It fascinates me to this day how we don't realize the cycle of suffering we create for ourselves. Many of us see ourselves as good people, but we often drive others away with our unconscious behavior. There is a disconnect in the way we imagine ourselves to be and how we actually are.

When I was sad, I went to the gym. Anticipation of Edward's compliments about my body accompanied me there. It was great motivation. He used to say that I should exercise to maintain my youth and keep my butt perky. The more he admired my body, the fonder of fitness I became.

In Brazil, a perky butt is the object of national adoration. It could almost be turned into a law, really. I remember at a very young age comparing myself with other girls who had a bigger butt. This competition was second only to which of us could *samba* better. Later, when I met my first husband and he introduced me to fitness through gym workouts, I quickly found proven methods to keep my butt perky. What a treat; it meant more compliments turned into feelings of self-worth. It also meant committing to the gym at least three times a week just to work on this body part. I recall being in the middle of a kickback session one day when a personal trainer came to me and said he had noticed I only worked on my lower body. He added that he'd be happy to help me with exercises for my upper body as well. My reaction was that of a growly dog when someone tries to take away his tasty bone. I politely said no to the trainer, but in my thoughts I was upset with him for trying to sabotage my source of happiness.

To illustrate how our sense of self is flexible and inconsistent, I changed the focus of my workouts from my lower body to my upper body a few years later. This happened when I began training like bodybuilders do—split-part workouts that emphasize a different body part every day. My upper body began to gain definition and receive attention. People began to compliment my upper body, and then of course I couldn't wait to get to the gym to train my upper body. I'd forgotten I was even born in Brazil.

MIAMI

It didn't take long for Edward to suggest we move in together. He talked about marriage and going to the United States. He said I could become a dance instructor in Miami, or dance at elegant venues. It would be a great opportunity to be discovered as an artist.

Everything sounded like a dream, except for the dancing/ artist part. I didn't know exactly what he meant by that. I didn't question it—I completely trusted him, although our tug-of-war on the subject of what was most important in life continued. Regardless, we prepared to move in together and got ready for our relocation to the United States in a few months' time. I hoped I would change his mind about love and he hoped he would change mine about art, fame, and money. Whatever happened, I thought it was worth the try.

I wanted to make sure Edward understood me better before we took these next big steps in life together. I wrote him a long letter in Portuguese and asked my English teacher to translate it for me. In my letter, my main message to him was that there was nothing more precious than what we had in our hearts. It was a long letter, but it was really repeating the importance of love and kindness in every line in different ways.

Edward read the letter and hugged me for a while. We were almost set to move to Miami. Before we left, there were two trips we had to make: one to my parents' home, and the other to Rio de Janeiro to get my visa. I had forgotten Sofia the same way she had forgotten me when she met someone who touched her heart.

Visiting my family with Edward would not be fun. I hadn't seen them in so long, but we had kept in touch by letters since I met Edward. They knew I was about to leave the country and were happy for me.

The visit went exactly how I expected. I counted the seconds until we could leave while Edward tried to figure out what part of my family I took after. My family was thrilled that I was marrying a "rich" man and moving to the United States.

When the day came to leave for Miami, I realized my life was changing again, but I wasn't sure how much of me was changing in a deeper sense. We arrived mid-morning at Miami International Airport. Edward and I stood side by side, close to the baggage carousel area. It was taking a long time for the rest of our luggage to arrive. We already had one piece, but there were three more to go. Lots of people were all around us.

I was quiet, looking around and keeping an eye on the carousel, when all of a sudden, I felt a hand give a heavy push to the back of my upper arm. I had to brace myself not to fall.

Confused, I looked around to try to find out who had pushed me and why. I looked at Edward. He was staring at a woman's butt. She was standing in front of me, and I had been blocking his view.

My reaction caught me off guard. I was so angry and offended that I slapped him on the face. His behavior didn't make sense to me—neither did my reaction, but I couldn't think clearly.

He screamed, asking if I had lost my mind.

"Seu sacana (You bastard)," I said aloud in Portuguese. I couldn't think in English anymore. "O meu amor por você não é suficiente? Eu faço tudo por você. Cadê o respeito? (Isn't my love enough? I do everything for you. Where is your respect for me?)" I looked into his eyes and tried to find a reason to remain with him after this.

I found plenty—mainly that I had no life without him.

In silence, he looked at me and rubbed his red face.

I sat down on top of one our bags, lowered my head, and closed my eyes. I saw flashes of Dara hugging and kissing my cousin while I worked hard for her affection.

Why am I seeing these images of the past? I thought. I opened my eyes and saw a couple with a little boy walking by. He was smiling and skipping, holding his parents' hands. I looked at the boy and wished I was him.

This marked the beginning of my new life with my first husband. We spent the first few months with Edward's family. They had a large home. While Edward was looking for a teaching job, I spent my days at home studying English on my own.

Everything fascinated me there—from the wide, open streets to the tall people and the large restaurant portions. I had the impression that size was the national trademark. I went back to the fish-eye talk. My English was not good enough to explain my beliefs and feelings, so I felt I could communicate better without words.

Edward's family thought I was too young for him, though I actually felt the opposite. But I couldn't use words to express myself to show them how much older than him I was. Silence became my language again, for the first time since my days in Bravo.

Edward found work in a private school soon after we arrived, and we moved to Miami Beach. I started taking English as a second language in school, and worked part time at the front desk for Gold's Gym.

Before my three-month visa expired, Edward and I got married. It was a simple wedding. Only a few people from his family were there. The day of our courthouse wedding, the faceless man from my dream was revealed to me in the moment Edward said, "Yes, I do." How fascinating to see a dream come true, at least one.

Life went on quite normally the next day.

DANCING

My part-time gym job ended around six p.m. Edward was already there when I got home. We usually went for a walk in the busy, touristy area of town. One day, we were walking on Ocean Drive, the avenue in South Beach that showcases rumba Flamenco dancers. There was a performance taking place. All the dancers had a Hispanic background, most of them from Spain.

Edward looked at me and said, "You could become one of these dancers; you dance better than them. I am sure you could get a job here."

I laughed a little, sure he was joking. My laughter had a short life span. He looked at me again and repeated what he'd said. We were standing among a crowd on the sidewalk in front of a restaurant, and it didn't take long before I felt the same sensation I'd felt that day in the Miami International Airport.

Edward pushed me forward. I found myself in the space between the people and the small stage where the dancer and guitarist performed. I stood there, petrified. Everyone was looking at me, puzzled, and Edward was screaming louder than the music.

"Dance, Valeria, dance—show them you are the best!"

The performers stopped playing and everyone stared at me. I lowered my head; my legs were heavy, but I found a way to move them so I could get back to where I'd been. I silently started walking away. Edward followed me. He kept asking why I was leaving and why I didn't dance. There were no words to express the way I felt. My confusion, embarrassment, and humiliation were too great.

At home, Edward tried to get into a conversation about it and scolded me for not dancing. We got into a fight. I had a hard time falling asleep.

My routine didn't change much for a few months, except that Edward suggested I add new classes to my curriculum in school. He said besides studying English, I should also take music lessons, so I started taking vocal and piano lessons. I thought about my father, who used to play the accordion and sing; perhaps the talent for music ran in my blood and Edward recognized it. At least it sounded more interesting to me than being pushed into the middle of a crowd to dance rumba Flamenco.

On one of those evenings on Ocean Drive, we saw a crowded restaurant where a solo Flamenco guitarist played. Edward rushed ahead of me. A crowd was slowly gathering by the restaurant's sidewalk to watch the performance.

I got there a few minutes later. I was standing by Edward's side when I felt the same violent push from a hand on my back. A strong feeling of betrayal and anger took over me as I found myself again standing in middle of a crowd, with Edward screaming like a mad man, "Dance, Valeria, dance!"

I stood there, unsure what to do. Should I run back home, get my things, and leave? Slap him on the face again? That was when I heard everyone in the crowd, about thirty people or more, say in unison, "Dance, Valeria, dance."

The guitarist, who had been sitting, stood and played louder, with more passion and energy. I felt the sound of each note he played reviving the cells of my body that had been about to die from anger. Blood was rushing through me; my body was feeling the music. Faced with the choice between running home and dancing, I started to dance.

I felt like a flame that becomes bigger with every blow of the wind. The crowd's shouting fueled my need to please them, and the music touched my soul, burning my pain. For a moment, everyone and everything around me disappeared. The music reached into my body with a fiery energy that aimed for the skies. It was a kind of known-yet-unknown sensation I'd never felt before.

I ended up on the floor precisely at the last note of the song. I was sitting with my legs crossed, almost in a lotus position. The crowd's screams were euphoric; the guitarist was clapping. Edward was screaming, and I had no idea where I had been or what I was doing on the floor with that last pose.

Edward came to me, kissed me, and helped me get up. He gave me his hand and bowed to the crowd. Before the crowd dispersed, a man wearing a fancy suit approached and invited us inside the restaurant. He guided us to the bar area and politely introduced himself as the manager. Two glasses of wine were handed to us.

He said that Gloria Estefan owned the place, and he knew she would be pleased with his decision to hire me as their exclusive rumba Flamenco dancer. The man shook my hand. He said he'd absolutely enjoyed my performance, and I could start working there the following weekend. The money was great. I could not believe someone would pay me to dance the way I did. I had no idea how to replicate that performance, but I knew I'd found a new way to celebrate my soul and burn my pain.

Life was the same for a while. I both worked part-time and exercised at the gym, went to school during the day, and danced rumba at night. I had new ways to be "happy," but my heart had no interest in the life I was living.

There wasn't any real communication with my family, aside from my arduous and persistent attempts to show them I was doing really well. When we talked briefly on the phone, they kept asking me if I was okay. I didn't understand why they would ask such a question, considering all the pictures I had sent of me dancing, smiling, hanging out alongside Gloria Estefan, eating at fancy restaurants, playing with my dog, relaxing at my comfortable apartment, being hugged by my husband, and traveling. I got angry every time—I guess I knew that they knew I wasn't okay, but they asked anyway just to annoy me. How could I be okay if I hadn't forgiven them? We all knew that true forgiveness and joy were close together.

What really bothered me was that I didn't have the courage to tell them that the pain from my past still held power over my real smile, the one not shown in those pictures. There was no hope in my marriage anymore. Edward and I had nothing to talk about or to do together. He was blinded, like most people, by fame and money.

CAN WE STILL MAKE IT?

Since Edward and I were drifting apart he made one last attempt to connect us. We added a new member to our sad family: Lilo, our Labrador puppy.

The day we went to get Lilo, something curious happened. On a sunny afternoon, we were in the backyard of a beautiful suburban home. We stood in the grass looking at ten puppies that were crawling around, displaying their cuteness. They were jumping on each other, playing with bones or coming near us to say hello. Most of the puppies were energetic and playful, except for Lilo—he was the only one in the corner of the yard, away from the others. He looked scared and lonely.

After spending almost an hour trying to figure out which puppy to choose, Edward picked Lilo. I was holding a playful, happy one, when he came to me with Lilo in his arms.

"This is the perfect puppy. I have been observing him all this time. He is calm and quiet, unlike the other ones. He doesn't bark and doesn't move much. He is more likely to obey me. Let's take him." How much I felt like that puppy!

At work, major changes were in progress as well. The guitar player I worked with had to go back to his country to attend to some family issues. The restaurant manager didn't hire another guitarist. Instead, they cut live entertainment altogether.

The day we got the news I wouldn't be dancing at the restaurant anymore, Edward had another idea for my artistic career. He said I could sing and become the next Latina pop star. Again and again, I wished he was joking—but instead of laughing, he added that he would find a music producer for me. If there was ever a time I should have left Edward, it was then; but I didn't.

At a cocktail party weeks before, Edward and I had been introduced to a well-known musician and music producer who lived in the area. The musician had given Edward his number.

So there I was, at a music studio. The producer was Juan. He was a young, talented Latin musician with a great work ethic. A few years back, one of his songs had become number one around the world, especially in Europe. He sang, played the guitar, wrote, and produced his own music.

You know the feeling when you are lost, but keep walking in any direction hoping you'll find your way? That was me. I had no idea what I was doing with my life at that point. I just hoped music would act as a stronger drug for numbing my pain than dancing and fitness.

Edward made a deal with Juan, and we started meeting at his studio three times a week to write and produce a demo song.

Meeting Juan was a scary, nerve-racking experience. Edward said I had great potential for music, but he often contradicted himself. When I was practicing at home, he would say I sounded horrible and that he could do a better job than me, except that he didn't look the way I did.

So my experience with Juan started out awful, even though he was such a patient and caring person. I feared every note he asked me to sing. In my mind, I could hear Edward's disapproval.

Juan noticed how insecure and frightened I was, so he was extra patient and nurtured me through the process. He was a great teacher who also became a friend. We talked about relationships, the music industry, and exercise, which he was also very much into. We laughed while eating olives. He could tell I needed help in my relationship with Edward, but he never mentioned anything. His prudence and professionalism made me trust him. But I still couldn't write any good melodies in his studio. I asked for a week on my own to come up with a melody. At the end of that time, I'd written a song titled "Always."

It was about my desire to see the outside world with my heart, since love was the only thing that was real to me.

Juan was surprised and enchanted by the song when I sang it for him. We started recording right away.

I had no idea I could sing or write music until I met him. But my relationship with music wasn't as freeing as dance was. There were too many technicalities involved—it required years of training to sing well. I had two months.

With Juan's incredible patience, the demo song was ready. Edward gave himself a new title: executive producer and manager of a rising pop star.

Before I could play music, music had to play my heart. Edward didn't understand what this meant. He listened to "Always" and immediately sent it to every major label in the United States. He also took me to many music events in the city, introducing me as the next Latina pop star. He set up a band and scheduled gigs around the city at small venues.

My short-lived experience as a musician began the way I started all my relationships—by trying to find the deepest and truest connection between us. I was starting to develop this connection to music, but it couldn't survive Edward's over-ambitious desires for money and fame. The possibilities for a deep relationship with music ended just so I could keep my shallow relationship with Edward out of fear.

For the next few months, I embarrassed myself by playing Latin pop sensation roles around Miami. We started receiving rejection letters from labels; there was no real money from the gigs; and our relationship was becoming more and more difficult. We fought constantly. It was a mess—a mess that Edward tried to clean up with another one of his ideas.

I woke up one morning to his enthusiastic new decision.

"Let's go to New York! There, you'll have many more chances to succeed as a singer."

With a yawn, I said yes as I got out of bed and walked to the bathroom. Edward spent the next few weeks applying for jobs in New York and booking apartments to see. There was a good chance that a private Jewish school would hire him. It was the beginning of the summer, and school started in September. He figured we would have time to find another job in case this specific school didn't hire him.

We sold most of our furniture and rented a U-Haul truck. We drove from Miami to New York with our sofa bed and a few other small items.

Less than a week before we left Miami for New York, I was coming from the gym on the bus when I started a random conversation with an old man sitting next to me.

"Where are you going?" he asked.

"To Collins Avenue. It's close," I told him, and turned my head to look at a man crossing the street with his cute dog.

"I mean, where are you going in life?" he said, looking at me.

I was surprised to hear a question like that from someone I'd never seen before. "I am moving to New York with my husband in a few days. Why are you asking this?"

"Do you love your husband?"

"I am grateful for all he's done for me. Isn't that love?" I said.

"I lived in New York for many years. There's one thing everyone should know about that place: It's a city for soul exploration, not love searching. I think you are still searching for love. I can see it in your eyes." He then quietly got up and prepared to get off at the next stop. But before he left, he wished me, "Bon voyage."

NEW YORK

It was early morning when we drove into Manhattan. We had an appointment at noon to see a small studio near Times Square. On the way, we stopped by Central Park. I couldn't stop looking up at those tall trees. Their top branches seemed to touch the heavens. Excitement took me over, and I was carried away by wonder.

It felt like I was being found after so many years lost. I had a feeling New York would be a new numbing drug for my pain.

The people around were young; just looking at them through the car window energized me. I watched them rushing to cross the street, as if they were about to meet the love of their lives on the other side.

After our driving tour, we met the young realtor at the studio at noon. The realtor opened the door for apartment 07. It took about a second to take the place in. A single window faced 8th Avenue, on 44th Street. There was a lot more to see out of the window than inside the apartment. The studio rent was high for a place that could hardly fit one person.

We left to talk about the deal. Standing outside on the sidewalk, Edward and the realtor discussed details. While they talked, I watched the doorman pet a resident's dog. He had a wide smile on his face. He greeted the lady kindly, then rushed to open the building's door for her.

The lady didn't smile back, and the dog didn't swing his tail. They went inside slowly and silently. The man went back to where he'd stood before greeting the lady and petting the dog. He held a stiff pose, with arms down and hands crossed in front of his body. He didn't seem so cheerful now that he was listening to his own thoughts. After seeing this, I had a feeling I shouldn't have been so excited about New York, though the food at the restaurant across the street seemed delicious.

We moved in that same afternoon. A few days later, Edward was hired by the Jewish private school. I also got a job at Gold's Gym, at the front desk. It was close to the apartment. Edward placed ads online looking for musicians to partner with me, musicians with experience who could put a band together to play around the city. It didn't take long to get dozens of replies. The musicians came to our apartment for auditions.

One of these musicians was Vicente, a tall man who seemed very familiar to me. Meeting him was like seeing an old friend.

He was a Bahian musician who had just returned to New York. A few months before, he had experienced a disastrous loss. He lost all his money and band to his business partner. Unable to deal with the incessant approaches from fans and fellow musicians asking what had happened to him, he returned to New York, where he had lived for a few years before starting his own band in Brazil.

Vicente was curious to know my potential as a singer and what kind of deal Edward had to offer. We talked about putting a band together, but the conversation bored me—all I wanted to do was to talk to Vicente about his sadness and try to help him feel better. We agreed to meet days later.

As he left the apartment, I watched him going down the stairs to the door and wished I was leaving with him.

FRESH BREAD AND HOT COFFEE

Vicente and I met at a music studio near Times Square where the other Brazilian musicians were rehearsing. Edward was working. Afterwards, we went for Italian food. Vicente and I found out we both very much enjoyed fresh bread. There was something about the way Vicente made me feel that I couldn't explain. His sadness was very attractive to me. I wanted to find a way to make him happy, but I was not interested in him as a man, only as a friend. He was a womanizer, the last man on Earth I would be with romantically.

Yet every time we said goodbye, I got the same feeling I'd had before at the door of my apartment, the first time I met him: I wanted to leave with him and not go back to Edward.

We started playing at Brazilian venues in New York. I was not connecting with music the way I would have liked to, but singing was becoming more natural to me. In the process, Vicente and I became inseparable friends. Being around him became my most enjoyable moments in New York—having bread and coffee with him after rehearsals, gigs, and whenever we felt like it. I wanted to be around him all the time, just not in a romantic way.

BREAKING THE DEAL

In one of our conversations, Vicente surprised me.

It was noon. We were at our favorite Italian restaurant, eating our favorite bread and drinking a tall cup of coffee, when Vicente asked me to run away with him to California. I spit coffee and couldn't stop laughing. I was sure he wasn't serious. I looked at him in fear that he was.

He said I had touched his heart, that I had made him smile in a special way. I explained to him that those feelings were normal and they would go away. We couldn't be together. It was not possible—not because I was married, but because I saw him as no more than a best friend. He looked down, went back to eating, and we didn't talk again about it. It was an awkward moment. It felt like our friendship was ruined. That day, when we walked away from each other, I didn't wish to go with him.

I went home and realized that his words had touched me with such power that I couldn't sleep for thinking about what he said. It explained the reason why, for the first time since we'd met, I hadn't wished to go with him. Somehow, part of me had already walked away with him.

Vicente became the center of my world after that day. I felt that our "souls" had been together throughout many lifetimes. We began a highly emotional relationship while I was in the midst of another one. Everyone in the band noticed that there was something going on. My marriage was about to end. Edward was becoming increasingly aggressive at home.

I didn't suddenly fall in love with Vicente—it was as though my "love" for him had been there since the first day we met. We both had a deep, painful relationship with ourselves. Although our lives had been surrounded by lots of people, and we would do anything to please others, we felt lonely most of the time. We shared the same intense desire for true human connection.

Days after Vicente and I started seeing each other romantically, I asked Edward for a divorce. He was furious and refused to do it.

I moved in with Vicente. We were making very little money with our gigs, and my part-time gym job was not enough to help with expenses. I got a full-time job at a luxurious hotel downtown. I worked long hours at the front desk and didn't have enough time or energy to sing on weekdays, only the weekends.

Soon, my relationship with Vicente started to change radically. His womanizing behavior, which I had completely forgotten, was making me jealous. We fought constantly. The more nights I spent alone, the harder I worked out at the gym.

To make things worse, Vicente decided to go back to Brazil for a few months to think about our relationship. He promised to stay in touch by email. During this time, we exchanged emails almost every day. When he came back, we started living together again. I didn't want to lose him this time, so I tolerated his womanizing behavior. We started playing again around the city.

Edward filed for divorce, claiming I had abandoned him and our home. I signed the papers, and we met briefly after that. He didn't look me in the eye. I knew we had been together for the wrong reasons. I felt like I had broken a deal with him, but not his heart.

I AM HERE FOR YOU

Vicente and I began to play more often and make more money. I quit the hotel job. We recorded some new demos I had written while he was in Brazil, including a song called "Peace." In the song, I wondered if we could find peace, or if peace would find us.

Everyone from the band, especially Vicente, started to believe more in my talent as a musician. They were intrigued by the music I wrote, the melodies, and the way I tried to express my feelings. This gave Vicente the idea of going back to Brazil with me. There, we could record an entire album of original songs. In New York, it was too expensive to do that. I agreed with him. Vicente had a house, so we wouldn't have to pay rent. All we needed to do was save as much money as possible for a few months, enough to stay there for six months while we recorded the album. Vicente's friends were well-known musicians, so we also had a studio to record at. I was excited about our new adventure. For him, it was a musical adventure; for me, it was love.

The day we left for Brazil, it was freezing cold. We were standing outside our building in Queens with our luggage, waiting for the cab. We could hardly see each other's faces; the wind blew snow fiercely. I had to tell him something before we got in the cab.

I told him that going to Brazil to record songs was great, but that the only music that mattered to me was the kind that played in our hearts.

He looked at me and said, "You are so romantic."

I didn't think he understood me, but it was too late now.

NOT WELCOME

When we arrived in Brazil, the cab took the coastline road to get to Vicente's house more quickly. I was convinced Vicente hadn't listened to me before we left New York. I looked at the vast ocean; the waves were pounding fiercely on the sand. It didn't seem to be welcoming me back.

We began to write songs the same week we arrived in Brazil. Our goal was to have at least twenty songs to choose from before we went into the studio. It took us about two months to generate over twenty song ideas. We recorded them with our limited home studio equipment.

My routine was writing songs, going out with Vicente to watch his friends perform, and going to the gym regularly and to the beach from time to time. I also cooked our food, cleaned the house, and practiced my vocal exercises. We spent time with Vicente's son and his family on the weekends.

I contacted my family to let them know I was back in Brazil. They never stopped asking me if I was okay. This was because I kept trying to show them I was. Telling them I was not fine would entail a long story that even I didn't want to hear. So I kept lying to them, and they kept annoying me with the same question.

After about three months, we began to record the songs, and my routine changed. In the mornings, I was now rehearsing songs with the band for a couple hours before going to the studio to record them.

Vicente's womanizing behavior got worse in Brazil. Before going to bed, we would have long conversations about it, and neither one of us could sleep well after that. I didn't want him to leave me the way he had before, so I tried harder to tolerate it. It wasn't working. I was compromising my integrity. It was time to do something about it. We were halfway done with the album when I made a decision.

It was late. My luggage was ready. Vicente had just arrived home from a gig. I told him that we couldn't be together romantically anymore. The way he behaved was hurting me too much.

As usual, he insisted there was nothing wrong with his behavior, that I was just too jealous and insecure to be his partner. I realized that talking to Vicente about our situation wouldn't change my decision. I still had some hope for us, but it was fading away with every word he said.

I sobbed as he watched me from a distance with a puzzled look on his face. He didn't seem to understand what was wrong in our relationship, why I was sad, or what he could do or say to make me feel better. I stopped crying, looked him in the eye, and told him I was leaving. I would be going back to New York.

He said I couldn't leave; we had an album to finish, and he had made commitments with the studio and band members. There was money invested, and his reputation was at stake.

He reminded me of Edward and his whole relationship-investment concept. It seemed like the men in my life invested everything but their hearts in our relationships. I suppose it was better to break deals than hearts.

I called his son to tell him the news and asked to stay at his place until I arranged my return to New York. His son arrived a few minutes later to pick me up. Vicente didn't want to talk to him. He was in the room, but stayed quiet as I left.

At dawn, we received a call. Vicente had been found lying down in the middle of a busy avenue. The police had taken him to a psychiatric hospital.

STUMBLED OVER THE TRUTH

As soon as I heard what happened to Vicente, I ran through the front door. I had no idea where I was going at that time of night. I was barefoot, wearing only a white nightgown.

I ran, and ran, and ran. I became aware of sand under my feet. I didn't know how long it had been since I started running. At some point, I slowed down to catch my breath and started walking. It was only semi-dark, as the moon illuminated the beach. My heart was getting lighter. I realized how long I had been out there when the sky started to change—the sunrise felt like an announcement of the arrival of God. I kept walking and finally sat down on one of the rocks where the waves crashed. I was waiting for God. There was an unusual feeling of serenity around me. My dress and body were getting wet; I didn't know if the water was coming from me, or if I was coming from the water.

I stayed there in silence for a while, watching the sunrise.

Why is there so much suffering? I asked the ocean, waiting for an answer.

Then I looked to the side and saw two birds standing on top of the rock closest to me. They looked identical. A new thought sprung up right away: The only reason I could see two birds is because of the space in-between them. If there were no space, the birds would be attached to each other and unable to fly.

Vicente came to my mind then. I remembered his smile when we went out to eat bread and drink coffee, when we played music together in Central Park, and when he told me that I gave him hope to believe in love again. What happened to the hope I gave to myself?

I smiled at the ocean and ran back home to take a shower and change. I was going see Vicente.

Looking at Vicente in the psychiatric hospital, it became clear to me that we humans are much more complex than we are able to understand. I realized in that situation that I knew very little about my own mind.

Without consistency of thought, Vicente had become somebody else, someone I'd never met. This was how I felt looking at him. He was someone I didn't know. Where was the Vicente I knew?

The doctor told me he needed to be medicated from then on. He'd suffered a panic attack, and his mental health would be compromised if it happened again. The only way to avoid irreversible brain damage was to keep him on medication. I didn't understand anything about mental problems, but to me the brain was an organ of the body like any other; it should be able to heal itself, like when someone has a heart attack. Patients take medicine for a while, but most of the time they also need to change their lifestyle, including exercising and eating a better diet. I realized that Vicente didn't behave the way he did because he was trying to hurt me; he simply didn't understand his own mind.

Vicente came home from the hospital a few days afterward. I'd decided to stay and help him recover. There were many changes to be made, but the first was already happening. My perception of life shifted. I became much kinder toward Vicente. I could see him not as someone who had hurt me, but as a man who knew very little about himself. It created a feeling of kindness in my heart.

I spent days researching how to treat mental problems naturally. There was a doctor from Canada, Dr. Abram Hoffer, who attracted my attention with his approach to mental health. He had healed thousands of patients using orthomolecular methods. A quote I read on his website intrigued me, and it made my decision to follow his guidance easier: "Man will occasionally stumble over the truth, but usually manages to pick himself up, walk over or around it, and carry on." - Winston S. Churchill.

I called Dr. Hoffer's office and talked to his assistant. They gave me a protocol to follow, which consisted of high doses of vitamins, especially niacin. The journey to help Vicente recover began. I cooked healthy, fresh foods, and he took all the vitamins and exercised every day. There was more space between us, too. I didn't question his behavior anymore. I gave him space to be himself. I didn't mind if he came home late or not at all after his gigs.

A few weeks later, Vicente was back to "normal." I felt much calmer around him and accepted our situation. There was a deep understanding that Vicente was trying his best, given how his mind worked.

The album was almost finished, but we had money issues. The new diet and his supplements were getting too expensive. I was going to have to look for a job, but how could I find a job that would allow me to take care of Vicente, the house, make music, and have time for myself?

"CLARO, EU FALO INGLÊS"

Coming back home from the gym, I realized there was an English school on the corner of the street. That's it, English, of course! I could speak English well, and I enjoyed it. I missed it, too. I could teach conversation lessons to beginners.

The next day, I put some formal business clothes on and headed to the school. I asked the receptionist there if I could apply for an English instructor position. She said yes, but I had to take the test. The school required all instructors to follow their method. The test was basically to see if instructors had the English skills to teach this method.

I took the test. It wasn't hard, but it was extremely technical. It was all about grammar, phrase structure—everything but pronunciation. Pronunciation is, to me, the melody of a language; how could I teach English without teaching pronunciation? I knew this job wasn't for me. I thanked the interviewer for her time and left.

I knew I could teach English conversation classes; I just needed to find out how. At home, the first thing I did was to go to the computer. I searched for schools in the city that only provided conversation lessons. In the search results, I saw various ads from private instructors. That was it—I had found the way!

I placed a number of ads for private conversation lessons on major websites. That same week, I had at least ten emails inquiring about my lessons.

Vicente was fine with students coming to the house. I set up a table and two chairs outside, so he still had his privacy. Students walked straight from the main gate to the side of the house without going inside. I provided water.

My first student was a shy, young businessman. His English was good enough to have a slow-paced, limited conversation. I asked him basic questions, and he answered. After a few lessons, I began to notice that a lot of the time the students and I were both staring at each other in silence. Either the subject was not interesting enough to hold our attention, or I didn't have any more questions to ask them. This was when I realized I needed a method.

So I created a written outline for the questions or subjects to talk about during the lessons. I came up with a method called "Let's Talk About ..." For each lesson, I had about ten to fifteen different topics. These were short paragraph excerpts of different subjects to discuss. A few weeks later, I felt much more confident during my classes.

Curiously enough, I only chose "how to live" topics. They were about love, courage, fear, hope, happiness, peace, and pain, among other deep topics. I also included topics about physical health, exercise, and diet. My lessons were a success. I became so busy I hardly had time for anything else. Later, I actually sold my method to some private English teachers around Brazil.

At the end of each lesson, most students said one of two things: Either, "I feel light. Time went by so fast I completely lost track of it." Or, "when I come here to see you, it doesn't feel like I am only taking an English lesson; I learn about life and spiritual things with you."

My time was well spent. I was making enough money to help with house expenses and to go out with Vicente on the weekends to buy stuff and eat at fancy restaurants. There were a lot more things to distract me from the sadness I felt about our relationship.

Music was not a career for me, and Vicente knew it. He was trying hard to accept it, but still insisted we shouldn't give up. We finished recording the album. Vicente tried to get a record deal with the local music labels, but nothing happened there. He watched TV during the day and went out at night. I was deeply unhappy with our relationship, but when I looked at him and saw him laughing at a silly scene in a movie, it made me smile.

THE BIG APPLE

One Saturday while I prepared to teach Joana, a psychologist who was one of my new students, she began by asking me a question.

"What are you doing here in Salvador? Since we met more than a month ago, you mention in almost every class how much you miss New York. You don't seem to be happy here, although we have meaningful conversations about life."

Before she finished her last sentence, my tears started to fall. I couldn't speak a word. I cried and cried from a deep unknown place inside of me. Until then, I'd had this horrible feeling that I was trapped in an invisible prison where no one else could see me. I felt I was not strong enough to release myself from it. It felt liberating to be seen.

How did Joana know? I thought I had been so very good at hiding it from everyone. I smiled all the time while talking about love and hope.

In silence, Joana held my hand. Our lesson time was almost over when I stopped crying and asked her for help.

We began to exchange English lessons for therapy sessions. No one knew about this but the two of us. She also introduced me to her women's therapy group on Sundays. There, I found out about "Biodanza," a group dance therapy class, and I also joined them.

For the next few months, I immersed myself in therapeutic practices. I became even more tolerant with Vicente at home. Therapy was making me strong, but I was not totally sure if it was in a good way. At last, I decided to stop all the therapy sessions and move back to New York.

I wasn't afraid of Vicente's reaction, but I was concerned. Vicente and I desperately wanted to be in loving relationships, but neither of us were prepared to be in one at that point in our lives. I talked to his son about my decision and asked his family to be prepared for what might happen. I also gave them all the diet and supplement protocols, and asked them to keep an eye on him.

I picked a weekday morning to tell Vicente about my departure. His son was with us, just in case he ran out. He was calm when he heard the news. I felt he was in a much better state with all the vitamins and the clean diet.

All the arrangements for my return to New York had been made; I had my plane ticket and a place to stay. A Brazilian neighbor in the building Vicente and I used live in in Queens had agreed to let me stay with her for a few weeks. Most of my students were going to continue to take their lessons by Skype and pay me through PayPal.

The day I left, Vicente was not around. He had left early in the morning to meet a friend. I guess he didn't want to see me leaving. His son took me to the airport.

I really believed I loved him and that he loved me. But we both had been hurt so deeply that we didn't know how to let go of the pain. Staying apart was the only way back to our own hearts.

I was back in New York. I had no other plans for my life aside from helping my students practice their English. Those heart-to-heart conversations brought me close to my soul every time. I'd realized then how much I aspired to relate and connect with others.

Liana, the Brazilian friend who let me stay at her place, had also been in painful romantic relationships. We talked for days about it. She was one of the kindest people I knew, but I couldn't stay in her place for too long.

Liana introduced me to a friend who lived close by. He had been thinking about renting out one of his rooms for very little. He didn't really need the money, but he had some trips coming up, and it would be good to have someone to take care of his place. The room was small but comfortable, and the location convenient.

I spent most of my weekends there, too. I taught about eight students, and around five p.m. I went to the gym. Among my dear student-friends there was Patricia, a heaven-sent gift to me. We had long conversations about everything that was happening in my life at that time. She listened, she cared, and she supported me in every way she could. Patricia was one of those beautiful mysteries of the universe. I often thought of her as a real angel disguised as a friend to help me.

I felt like an old lady who needed rest. My room became my sanctuary. I mostly spent weekends there, too. I had no reason to be out in the world when my cozy little room made me feel safe. I felt like I was in some sort of rehab, recovering from a lifelong heartbreak.

LET ME LOVE

I received news that Vicente had been hospitalized again. He was in a psychiatric clinic after another mental breakdown. His son and family were overwhelmed and disturbed; they couldn't take care of him. They believed the best thing to do was to rent out Vicente's house and pay a mental institution to care for him.

I couldn't let this happen. I had to find a way to help him, so I spent the week contacting the hospital to speak to him directly. He was medicated. The doctor didn't allow him to come to the phone.

When I finally talked to him, over a week had passed since he had been hospitalized. He was still confused. I asked him to come back to New York so I could take care of him, but he was disconnected from our conversation.

On another phone call, he was much more clearheaded. He talked to me about how cruel the staff were and said he was being treated like an animal. They tied him up on the bed at night before giving him medicine, as they laughed and made comments about his skinny legs. He told me the food was terrible and everyone in the place was crazy, not just the patients. It made me sick to my stomach. I had to help him.

It occurred to me that the more specialized professionals are, the more problems are created, especially in the psychological domain. These professionals lose their ability to see life as a whole, especially a human life and its depth. It made me reflect on what a healthy mind is. How can somone see only one way of solving problems, especially human suffering? That is a problem we should all be able to understand and relate to.

The mental institution staff treated Vicente worse than the staff of a veterinary clinic would treat a sick animal. It seems as though when a human being loses his mental clarity around us, he becomes a threat to our own sanity. We don't want to be reminded of how fragile our minds are.

I said goodbye to Vicente and promised to call again the next day. From that day on, I called and spoke to him every day. I wanted to make sure the hospital staff knew he had someone who loved and cared for him.

When I called the hospital late one afternoon, they told me Vicente had been given permission to leave. The next call I made was to his son. Vicente was staying with him, and he was feeling better.

A week later, Vicente arrived in New York. He called me right away. There we were again in an Italian restaurant, eating fresh bread and drinking coffee. It felt like together we had awakened from a nightmare that had lasted years. We didn't talk about what had recently happened to him. Instead, we laughed about silly things, like how stiff and serious the waiter looked while serving us food.

Vicente looked different. He was very thin and pale, and his voice was weak.

My heart wanted to embrace him with all the love I had and never let go. Watching him eat and enjoy the food was heavenly to me. He was safe, and I made a promise to stay around him from then on.

My roommate was traveling, so I invited him to visit the apartment. I wondered if my cozy room would give him the same warm feeling it had been giving me. We ended up spending the entire week in my apartment. Then we began to look for an apartment to live in together.

I felt as though I was more prepared to love him, and at the same time take care of myself. My heart was filled with kindness for him for the horrible things that had happened to him. There were no expectations or desires to change him.

Everything happened fast after that week. We found a small, one-bedroom apartment in Queens and moved in together. He began to play with Brazilian bands around the city. I still had a good number of students for my Skype lessons, so I spent my days teaching and going to the gym.

It didn't take long before I realized I was reliving the same situation as when we were in Brazil. He watched TV during the day and at night was off at gigs. I would look at him laughing about something on TV, relaxed, lying there on the sofa eating a bag of chips, and I felt incredibly good. I would rather see him watching

TV here than staring at the ceiling of a psychiatric hospital room in Brazil.

THE PROMISE

We legalized our pain. I saw our marriage as a serious commitment to learn how to love Vicente and myself at the same time. The money we were making was not enough for the rent, to eat healthily, and pay for supplements, so he sold his house in Brazil. He bought a couple of black cars and opened a company, driving one of the cars and renting the other. In less than a month, we were doing incredibly well financially. I now needed to find a way to tolerate our painful marriage. Exercise was not cutting it anymore.

My despair was much more contained and silent than Vicente's had been.

The teachings of a guru from India who lived in Portugal drew me into the practice of deep meditation. I felt I had found the answer. I quit the gym and spent most of my days reading spiritual books, taking care of the house, teaching English lessons, and meditating. My guru's videos kept me company when I was alone. This was my real life. My marriage was a promise I'd made to keep Vicente away from the hospital.

I was watching one of my guru's videos that he made in his ashram in Portugal. He was sitting on a wooden chair. The place was clean and simple. A window showed the view outside, and there were beautiful trees and flowers all around the ashram. People, sitting on the floor, surrounded him. Everyone was attentive to his words. They had a peaceful smile on their faces. Another video showed them eating vegetarian food and delighting in deep conversation. I felt this was the place for me.

The decision was instant. I was going to live there and work for my guru. I felt I had found the answer. Vicente would be fine in New York. He was busy enough with his car company and playing music with his friends at night.

I had to break my promise.

On the same day I watched the video, I told Vicente about my decision while we were having dinner.

His expression instantly changed. He didn't finish his food and left without saying a word. A feeling of doubt and fear arose in me. My appetite was gone and so was my certainty about a life that a moment before had seemed perfect for me. My memories of Vicente hospitalized came back. I didn't want to go away and then get the news he wasn't well. It would keep drawing me back to him and my old life. Not knowing what to do, I went back to my room to meditate for the rest of the day.

FITNESS UPGRADE

I settled for my own ashram in my room.

A few days later while searching for new videos of my guru to watch, I came across a fitness competitor. It was a motivation video for anyone who wanted a body transformation. In the video, the competitor explained how important changing your diet was if you wanted to transform your body, and also how hard you have to train. I made precise notes. I had no intention to compete, but I thought maybe if I couldn't change my life, I could try transforming my body. The feeling of peace I got from meditation was great, but it also felt like I was closing my eyes to reality, hoping it would hurt less. I thought that at least with my workouts, my self-esteem would be high, which was a much more powerful numbing drug for all kinds of pain.

In the six months since I had found my guru, I'd gained more than ten pounds, and it was a nightmare to sleep with Vicente after his late night gigs. I was 5'4" and 138 pounds. I couldn't see any muscles in my body; my self-esteem was low, and I had stopped looking at myself in the mirror.

I wondered if having a body like that woman was really possible. I would find out. I was about to make a comeback to fitness in a way I never had before.

I started on my plan for a new life. I got up, went straight to the kitchen, and threw away all the refined, processed, and sugary foods. I was ready to go out food shopping and to sign up for the gym.

I got dressed. All my clothes were super tight, and trying to hide the extra pounds was tough. Leaving the house was even tougher. I thought of Ana and her detective walk—how could I get to the supermarket and the gym without being seen? How could I avoid the laser stares from people, targeted at the fat around my belly? Nothing could stop me from starting my "body transformation" program that day. I left the house armed with my new workout routine and shopping list on my phone.

How hard could it be to get in shape again?

I got to the gym and asked the front-desk person about the fees. While she was looking on the computer, I got a cold feeling in my stomach. Every single thought I had about the place was negative. The gym seemed too big, too open, too dark. The music was too mellow, the stretch room too crowded, the girls there too thin, and on and on. My mind was looking for ways to sabotage my plans. Then, when the receptionist told me how much the membership was, another thought jumped in—too expensive. My last words to her were, "Thank you very much!"

It felt great to walk away from that place. What a relief. But I still had to find a place to work out. I was letting fear win. I couldn't anymore, not at that point in my life. I turned around and signed up.

My first body transformation workout felt great in the end. Walking back from the gym, I felt much better. I even thought I could stay with Vicente forever. I went by the health food store and bought all the items I needed to prepare my own muscle-building meals.

But my new life plan wasn't new at all. I was finding new ways to keep my old self alive.

My workout routine had changed drastically. Before, I used to wander the gym looking for lower body machines, then bike for a while. I was not working out like bodybuilders do, using split-part training. Each day of the week, a different muscle group gets a pump.

In less than five months, I resembled a fitness competitor—not exactly like the woman in the video that had inspired me, but close enough. My self-esteem was high. Vicente was glad I'd changed my mind about going to Portugal to live near my guru in the mountains. He was not going out as much. My husband was even buying me flowers and taking me out to dinner more often.

I became popular at the gym. People complimented me and asked when I would compete. I had no intention of competing at all, but the comments were so frequent that I began to think about it.

"SORE SOUL"

At the gym, my conversations revolved around exchanging workout and diet tips. I never talked about my personal life and was not interested in anyone. I felt Vicente and I were doing better after my body transformation. I could spend the rest of my life with him this way. The results of my workouts were more potent than ever: I could endure emotional pain that much longer.

What I didn't know was that everything was about to change again.

During one of my training sessions, I met Ray. He was a shy young man who looked like a bodybuilder.

An older man came over to me and asked a question about deadlifting, an exercise I often practiced. He wanted to know about techniques. I saw Ray deadlifting a rack away from me, and told the man, "Ask that guy over there. He sure seems to know more about deadlifting than I do."

Ray was lifting a massive amount of weights for his size.

The man went over to talk to Ray. Moments later, he called me over, and Ray and I introduced ourselves. That day, we talked for a long while.

I thought that I had no feelings or curiosity about this man Ray. I admired his hard work. But there was that familiar something about him that I had felt with Vicente. I didn't know what it was. It was too subtle to analyze or think about, but powerful enough to make me forget my workout routine at the gym and go straight to Ray. There was nothing romantic going on—we would talk about everything except our personal lives. He made me laugh like no one ever had.

Vicente was going to the same gym, and didn't mind seeing Ray and I engaged in long conversations. He knew I was a faithful wife. What he had forgotten was that I was much more faithful to my romantic heart.

For months, talking to Ray at the gym was innocent fun, but my thoughts and feelings were starting to change. Every time I went to sleep, thoughts of Ray populated my mind.

One late night, Vicente came home from one of his gigs and tried to touch me. I pushed him away, turned on the light, and, looking straight in his eyes, told him I was in love with Ray, the man I'd been talking to at the gym. It came right out of my mouth that way. I couldn't hide my thoughts from Vicente anymore. It didn't feel right.

Vicente was shocked. I guess he didn't expect me to say anything like that to him. He didn't say anything. He walked to the bathroom and stayed in there for a while. Then he came back and shouted, "You think he is better than me? You're wrong. He won't put up with your desire for a 'perfect love'. No man will."

That night, Vicente slept in the living room and I couldn't sleep at all. Vicente had been one more pain I had embraced as my own. I wanted to find out the truth. *What pain is real? What pain is really mine?*

I ran to the gym the next day filled with excitement. I would tell Ray what I felt for him. The gym was quiet when I got there. Ray was working out in the back, by the heavy weights. I asked if we could talk for a moment. We sat on a bench nearby. It took minutes of deep breathing and silence before I could say anything. He was patient, but also anxious for my words to come out.

I finally said that I'd never felt so in love before, and that I couldn't stop thinking of him. My last words fell into a deep, vast silence. I could tell what I had just said touched him, but he didn't know what to do with it. He said he was surprised and didn't expect all of that at once. To make the uncomfortable situation a bit lighter, I told him not to worry; it might just be an infatuation. It would go away. However, secretly, the word "infatuation" bothered me.

He replied that I didn't know the meaning of the word "infatuation." He sounded defensive. I kissed him on the cheek and walked away. My life started to change rapidly again after that.

I decided to become a personal trainer and registered for a fitness competition. Vicente was moving out. Ray and I could not see or talk to each other outside of the gym until I got my divorce papers. He made this rule, which I thought was honorable.

Three months later, the divorce papers arrived and so did my trainer certification.

I called Ray to tell him the great news.

We started to see each other. As a woman of forty, I found myself contriving childish rules to direct my actions, like a lovestruck teenager navigating the dating world for the first time. Overrun by infatuation, I let my mind take me straight into another painful relationship.

It might be funny to you, as it is to me now, but during this period I wasn't aware of my behavior in romantic relationships. I believed I was being spontaneous—simply being myself. I was not ready to express the nature of true love rooted in kindness. It fascinates me how much of our own minds we don't know, and how much of the so-called rational mind's reality doesn't make any sense.

Since the beginning of my "infatuation" with Ray, I had a strange feeling my life was repeating itself. However, in a few months, there was no relationship with Ray anymore—not that we'd ever really had one.

So I started focusing on my new, exciting, and "successful" personal training career as well as fitness competition shows. At least with my career I was heading in the right direction ... or was I?

PART TWO

FROM FITNESS TO
DEPRESSION

Chapter 4

Training Clients in New York

THE SNOWFLAKE

A man walked into the fitness studio. He was out of breath. He stomped his boots on the floor to rid them of snow, and hung his long winter coat and hat on the half-full rack by the entrance.

He reached into his coat pocket, and a cigarette box fell to the floor. He picked it up and quickly put it back. His red eyes were wide and out of focus, scanning the room from end to end. He was clearly looking for someone.

It seemed to be a challenge for him to fit his body on the small sofa by the entrance. He adjusted himself many times. He reached for a fitness magazine on the coffee table in front of him and put it back a few seconds later to take the newspaper instead.

This man was my new client, David. He was thirty-nine years old, a well-off businessman who owned properties in Manhattan. He weighed over 300 pounds. I'd been waiting for him. He was on time.

"Good afternoon! You must be David," I said in a relaxed tone, with a smile.

"Good afternoon, Valerie. It's a pleasure to meet you," he said, looking at my arms. Immediately, he asked me, "How do you pronounce your name?"

"You can call me Valerie, it's fine. But if you like challenges, try 'Va-LÉ-ria.'" I smiled. He tried it a couple of times and gave up. A young woman walking on the treadmill nearest to us turned her head to look at us a couple times.

"So, Valerie ... I am here because I am interested in your mind," he said. "How do you get your body to obey your mind's best intentions and goals for your life? I want to know how you do this. There's something you must understand: I am very good at what I do. I am smart, driven, and I make lots of money. It's not a hard thing for me to be successful in this area, while for most people this is a really difficult thing.

"My problem is my habits. I love unhealthy foods, overeat, sit around a lot, and only sleep a few hours per night because I like going out to drink after work. I wasn't always this way. I used to be thin; I had an active lifestyle in my teens, even ate kind of healthy. My old friend, John, was my hero growing up. He was a basketball athlete. John's training routine, diet, and discipline were an inspiration to me."

David had to fight for air as he spoke. He lowered his head briefly, resting his forehead on his hand. He reminded me of a traveler returning from a wonderful trip to find himself in despair, wishing to return to the place he just came from. David was lost in his thoughts—someone whom he was once proud of seemed to be revisiting him. There was a moment of silence between us.

We both looked at an ESPN magazine lying on top of the coffee table, Kevin Love on the cover. The woman on the treadmill stepped off and passed us, wiping the sweat from her face as if she wasn't paying attention to our conversation. I knew David needed my help to lose weight and get healthy, but I wasn't sure what he really wanted from me. I kept listening to him without saying anything. The assessment session protocol I normally followed became a conversation about understanding what he was trying to achieve.

After a moment of reflection, he said, "Here's the deal, Valerie. I am intrigued by your mind and the way it focuses on healthy habits, discipline, and gets your body to look the way it does. Teach me how you do that, and in exchange I will teach you how to become a millionaire."

I looked at David, not knowing what to say. What he'd just said didn't make sense to me. I managed to say to him, "Dear David, you are allured by physical fitness, but in truth, what we are all searching for is a clear and serene mind—a way of thinking that is guided by your heart. When we make our hearts the master, our thoughts gravitate toward essential, meaningful purposes. We start seeing life as a wonderful journey, regardless of all suffering. Our thoughts then become the creators of life's most important purpose, which is to be happy.

"If you can teach me how to become rich while having a healthy heart full of joy and peace, we have a deal. I must also add that physical fitness has not turned me into a happy and serene person; I assume money didn't do it for you, either."

Our conversation ended with both of us watching the snow. Silent flakes drifted from the sky to the pavement. White and pure, they performed the most entrancing dance before melting on the ground to become mud. In that moment, I was no longer sure if we were watching the snow or it was watching us.

A few minutes later, the door closed behind David. He descended the steps slowly. I watched the snow and David become one as he walked away from the fitness studio, and from me.

David called me a week later. "When will we go out on a date to talk about that deal?"

* * * *

My life as a fitness trainer and competitor was a success, but I was not happy at all. Although my clients were paying me well and I seemed to be doing something positive with my life by helping others to improve their health, the world I'd built on the bricks of physical fitness was about to crumble.

Not long after I became a trainer, I realized my clients needed much more than physical fitness to be "healthy." They were no different than me. They wanted happiness, which exercise and diet couldn't promise. While training clients' bodies separately from their hearts, I felt I was being trained, too. My interactions with them turned me toward a doorway through which I'd find the real meaning of fitness and health, and begin an inner path of discovery.

The following stories, arranged as though they happened over one day, are about my relationships with my clients. Their disappointments and dissatisfaction were crucial in taking me to the depths of my own heart, which turned into a compassionate adventure toward others and myself.

* * * *

I met my first client of the day at seven in the morning.

Angela was a thirty-five-year-old married woman living in Manhattan. I reached her building thirty minutes early, and waited for her for another ten. When she arrived in the lobby to greet me, I remember wondering why she'd hired me. She was petite, young, and in great shape.

We walked to the gym, which was empty. She turned on the air conditioning and the lights. Our session began and we went through the initial protocol, a dynamic warm-up.

She looked down the entire time. I asked her unimportant questions to break the silence, but her answers were brief, accompanied by a shy smile. I felt my presence was enough for her. Throughout the workout, Angela only spoke a few words, moved in a slow, controlled way, and never looked straight at me. I felt like I was at a funeral and I didn't know who the dead person was. I felt awkward, trying to cheer her up or at least alleviate the silence. I pretended I was participating in a comfortable and normal situation between two people.

When the workout ended, we planned our weekly schedule and said goodbye to each other under the same gloomy cloud. This was a client whom the best exercise and diet in the world would never help to feel joyful. It was never about fitness for Angela. She was looking for a friend.

I left her building feeling very down. I couldn't pretend to be her warm friend while also being a trainer. Her sadness was my sadness.

There was no time to be unhappy, though. My next client was James, and he needed me downtown at ten. I crossed the street and entered the subway station.

When I met James for our first assessment session a few weeks back, in the same private fitness studio in downtown Manhattan where we'd be meeting today, he said to me, "I want to look like you." I remember hoping he meant to look fit and healthy, not ripped and starving while wearing high heels, as I was in my online competition pictures. James had found me through my website, where I'd posted these images.

He needed to lose about twenty pounds. Taking care of his health seemed to be a priority for him. However, he mentioned he had just broken up with his girlfriend, and that his main goal was to get in shape before joining a dating website.

I was meeting him for our fifth session.

"How are you feeling, James?"

"I am very well," he replied, but there was a sad look in his eyes that told a truth his words wouldn't. His heart was broken.

"Great, let's get started." I gave him some warm-up exercises. James was an easygoing, friendly person, and I instantly felt comfortable talking with him about matters of the heart. So I asked him, "What is the meaning of life to you?"

"What a big question for a Monday morning," he said, trying to concentrate on his plank hold. After a moment, he added, "I think the meaning of life is to be happy."

"What makes you happy?" I asked, curious.

"I'd like to have my girlfriend back," he said, looking at the floor.

"So your girlfriend gives meaning to your life?" I ventured, trying to express my doubt.

He was quiet for a moment. We moved on to the squat rack. Eventually, he said, "Well, for that, she needs to understand me better and love me for who I am." He looked at himself in the mirror and squeezed his belly.

"What do you mean by that?"

"I mean, that way she would complete me and I would be happy. I like having someone to share my life with. The special moments, you know? Someone to travel with, talk to, sleep with, go out to dinner with, and maybe have a child with. A partner. This is who I am. I'm used to being with someone. It's tough being alone."

James's last sentence didn't make sense to me. "In my opinion," I told him, "knowing who you really are requires being alone. Being with other people because we are used to it is only another way to escape from knowing ourselves."

How ironic it was that I needed to hear that, too!

By the time I'd finished sharing my thoughts, James had squatted for ten minutes. He'd burned quite a lot of calories, and had his hand on his chin in *The Thinker's* pose. I left our session hopeful, wondering if he'd understood what I'd said and pondering it in my own thoughts as well.

Before our meeting the week after, he sent me his picture. He was standing in front of the mirror and showing his belly. The message read: Look, Valeria! I have lost three pounds already and my belly is looking smaller. You are amazing! I am going to sign up for a dating website today—I am tired of being alone! I will see you later.

My next appointment was with Destiny at noon.

She called to say she would be almost twenty minutes late. I stared out at the street from the studio. There were many things going through my mind that day, even though my feeling of unhappiness was not connected to any of them. It was cold and windy outside, and I expected Destiny to come rushing in any minute.

Destiny was one of the most cheerful clients I had. She always went straight to me with a big smile, and gave me a tight hug and a kiss before we started training. She was a mother of two kids, taught school, and was overweight. Destiny was a high-energy woman with a very unusual fitness goal: to lose belly fat only. She trained with me three times a week.

When we met two months ago and I asked her about her fitness goals, she told me her husband would love to see her with a smaller belly, wearing the new pink swimsuit he'd bought for her that summer. She shook a colorful water bottle and took a sip, adding that she knew she was a bit overweight, but she liked her voluptuous body—except for her belly fat. Her husband had said all she needed to do to look great was lose belly fat.

It was not the first time I'd heard this kind of fitness request from a client, and I was used to it. I proceeded to explain to her that spot reduction was not possible with exercise and diet, and that while working out with me, she'd lose fat in her body overall, not only around her belly. Despite this, she was excited to get started. I don't think she understood me.

We started training from that day on. She was doing great. Destiny had lost almost twenty pounds so far.

After a long, melancholic wait by the window, she came rushing in. She looked serious and worried. It was the first time she didn't greet me with a hug and kiss. I hoped nobody had died.

We sat down on the sofa in reception. I faced her, but she looked down. She said she'd wanted to meet me in person to say something important. She didn't want to send an email.

"What's wrong?" I asked.

She said she couldn't do it anymore; I had helped her reduce her belly size and feel better, but she'd noticed that her thighs and buttocks were shrinking, too. It wasn't what she'd expected. She was looking down the whole time, about to cry.

I listened to her quietly. I didn't have much to say.

Destiny thanked me, then stood up and walked away.

My unhappy feelings from earlier now had a reason to hang around for the rest of the day.

Susan had a session with me at two in the afternoon. I was not feeling well after the encounter with Destiny. During lunch, my thoughts had been much more centered on love and kindness, and this reflection was hovering over me when Susan arrived. She'd been training with me for a couple of months.

I began chatting with her about these tender reflections. In the middle of our session, I said, "Susan, you know what I've begun to realize?"

"What?" she asked.

"That the foundation of health is love; how can we feel comfortable in our bodies if we are not in love with life? Does that make sense to you?"

She looked at me as if she was thinking about it. Then she said, "Valeria, can you please get the mat for my next buttocks workout?"

We continued with the session as if I'd never brought up the insignificance of a fit body without a loving heart and a happy mind.

Diana was next. We met at five in the evening.

She came in ten minutes early and hustled past me on her way to the locker room, saying, "It's been another busy day. Give me the hardest, most beast-mode circuit you've got, Valeria."

My energy was very low at this point. I really didn't want to train another client, especially a high-energy person like Diana. She was thirty-four-years-old and exercised every day in the morning before she went to work. Her jogging sessions lasted an hour. She usually met me in the late afternoons for her weight training.

Today was an upper-body session. While she lay under a sixty-five-pound loaded barbell, doing twelve reps of military presses, I asked her, "What is the most important thing in life to you, Diana?"

She was so focused on her reps that I wasn't sure she'd heard me. As usual, she was having a serious conversation with the barbell. We didn't tend to talk much. Her workout mood had always been to get the job done as well as possible and then leave the studio.

A few seconds later, she put the bar back on the rack. The next exercise was ab work, and she knew it. We had the circuits programmed in advance. She moved briskly to the yoga mat on the floor to do a set of twenty reverse crunches.

Her breathing was heavy. The circuit was intense. She was never happy with anything light or easy. I was still waiting for an answer to my question as I kept track of the number of reps, but I didn't ask it again.

On the floor, while doing a quick stretch - bending her knees close to her chest while keeping her legs together - she said, "The most important thing to me is to keep moving forward through the days. When I wake up in the morning, I have a to-do list in my mind. I just go through it naturally. It's a clear, focused, and precise daily plan I accomplish by the end of the day." She finished her answer by the assisted pull-up bar, after fifteen reps.

Diana had been moving fast for the last thirty minutes. She performed all her exercises with the same focus and precision as she checked off her to-do list.

"Do you like your job?" I asked.

She was so focused on her spider plank that her favorite movie star would have gone unnoticed had they walked by us. Sitting on the mat, wiping her face, she said that she got her job done, made great money, and was proud of herself. She worked out hard in one of the best fitness clubs in New York, and could afford my high personal training fees. She laughed and added that she ate out all the time, travelled, and went out with friends for drinks; serious relationships and love were too complicated to give attention to.

You know that feeling when there's nothing you can say to someone because they're too busy listening to their own thoughts? That's how I felt.

After we finished the workout, I reflected on how Diana's life was not much different from her to-do list. It was programmed. She'd been in a cycle of living according to rehearsed habits, and her life had turned into a running race with no finish line or winners, an existence driven by nonstop actions. There was no space left to even think about love.

Diana followed the exercise program and ate clean while training with me. She achieved the fit and athletic look she wanted in three months. Her body composition transformed, but I wish her life had, too.

My six o'clock client was not a regular. A fellow female trainer needed to leave because of an emergency and asked me to take her client that day. I filled in for her as a substitute trainer.

Steve was a fifty-seven-year-old businessman who seemed to be under a great deal of stress. I could tell this just by being around him for a few seconds. He gave me a serious, almost intimidating, impression, and breathed heavily. We were introduced in a hurry by the other trainer as she ran out the door.

Steve looked at me with an expression of quiet impatience. He was in good shape and looked strong. His chest area was well developed, leading me to think he must have been lifting heavy weights for years. I could tell he was very proud of his chest.

Before I could ask him about his training routine, he gave me the workout for that day. His program had only four exercises: barbell bench press (155 lbs. — 12 reps), incline chest press (50-lb. dumbbells — 12 reps), floor push-ups (20 reps), and incline dumbbell flies (20 lbs. — 12 reps). If you understand something about muscle-group training, you will notice that Steve's workout had only chest exercises.

I looked at his program and said enthusiastically, "Great! Let's do it!"

I set up the barbell and began the first workout on the list. I was ready to spot him if he needed it, standing close to the bench behind his head. As he ended each rep, I cheered him on by saying things like, "Great job, Steve. You've got it! Nice work! Keep up the energy! You can do it! Wonderful! You are doing it right! Don't give up! One more left! Nicely done!"

In truth, I was talking to myself. I needed to hear my own enthusiastic words, given the day I'd had. I noticed something unusual when I took a quick glance at Steve's face to make sure he was okay. He was looking at me and smiling as he lifted the heavy weight. He'd finished lifting without saying a word, but with a smile. I didn't exactly understand the reason for his happiness, but I was glad his serious and stress-filled expression was gone.

Considering he was a new client, I didn't feel comfortable enough to begin a conversation about my early insights into fitness and kindness. Nonetheless, I asked him trivial questions, which he didn't answer. I don't know about you, but I enjoy interacting with others when I'm with them. I like separating things: There is a time to be fully alone, and a time to be fully with others. In a trainer/client relationship, there are moments to focus on the exercise, moving and breathing properly, and also moments when we can talk.

Steve's behavior was making me feel incredibly awkward. Concerned but trying to stay cool, I followed him around with my cheerful chatter. His behavior didn't change. The studio was quiet; there were only a few people working out with their trainers. No one seemed to notice how uncomfortable I was around Steve.

Once again in my life, I felt stuck. I didn't want to stay there, but I couldn't leave. I tried to stay calm and do my job well.

We went through the workouts. In the end, Steve was sweating, still with a smile on his face. Before we said goodbye, he asked for my name again, then mentioned that he liked my training style. He also inquired if I could train him from that day on. I politely explained to him that my schedule couldn't fit another client.

In truth, if my heart had not begun to guide me toward fitness and spirituality, I would have accepted his offer.

Karen was my last client for the day. We met at seven sharp, right after Steve.

Karen was an obese woman I trained twice a week. She was thirty-years-old, weighed 250 pounds, and was 5' 2". However, these numbers don't say anything about her. She was a painter who owned her own gallery in Manhattan. The serenity in her eyes and the way she smiled for no reason introduced her before she even told me her name.

She had been married for more than five years to someone who was in good shape. I knew this because her husband came to pick her up after our sessions. The conversation we had the first day we met left me pondering about life for days.

I asked the same question I asked every client before we began the program: What are your three main fitness goals?

Karen said she only had one goal: to enjoy the workouts.

I recall looking into her eyes as if she had not understood my question. I rephrased it, and this time I was more specific.

"I understand, Karen, and I will ensure the exercises will be fun, but what I meant was, how many pounds do you want to lose?"

Again, she answered with a smile and said she didn't care about the weight; she just wanted to feel good during and after the workouts. Furthermore, she said it didn't matter if she didn't lose any weight at all. Her peaceful eyes and joyful smile reinforced the truth of her words.

I could not believe this woman and how out of touch with reality she was. She was obese, for God's sake! She could actually die of a heart attack at any moment, and my mind refused to believe that anyone could be at peace with a body like hers. It couldn't be possible.

I insisted. I tried to force her to make a deal with me, and asked her to agree on losing one to two pounds per week.

With the same serene, happy look on her face, she replied that I didn't understand her. Patiently, she repeated that she was fine with her weight and that she enjoyed her work. She was a person who loved and was loved by her family and friends. Her life was a blessing, and she was grateful for what she had. There was nothing else to be added or removed to make her happier. The workouts with me were just to get her body moving while she had some fun.

I wasn't amazed by her attitude, because I neither understood nor believed in what she was saying at the time. Nevertheless, after our encounter that day, I went home thinking about her, and I remembered a thought I'd had when I was a teenager, one that had returned many times throughout my life.

I would die young.

I believed I would not reach the age of thirty, despite being physically healthy.

Perhaps intuitively, I knew that my heart could fail at any time because of my lack of understanding of what life was really about: love and kindness.

I am convinced that Karen became my client for a reason—to teach me that to be healthy is to be loving. She trained with me for almost a year, and never lost any weight.

Karen was the healthiest client I ever had.

* * * *

I became a personal trainer in my late thirties after years of living the fitness lifestyle. It was a simple and easy transition; for years, I had been helping those around me reach their fitness goals for enjoyment. If there was any time to embrace a new career, it was after my second divorce, followed by the disastrous infatuation with Ray. I felt like my romantic life had come to a dead end. It was time to put all my energy into other areas, in the hope I would find that ever-desired land of happiness.

I registered to participate in a fitness competition and got a job in one of the largest fitness club chains in the country. While preparing to compete and gaining experience at a well-established fitness club, I built a website. In less than two months, my website began to attract a great number of visitors; they were potential clients who had found my ad somewhere online. My new career was starting to thrive; I was training six to seven clients per day and making great money. I felt stronger than ever, physically and emotionally. I really believed all was well and that I had overcome major challenges in life with the power of action and my ability to move forward. I'm sure you've heard about people who seemed to be well, happy, and normal, then one day they either suddenly stayed in bed with depression or they killed others or themselves. I was heading toward one of these horrible events, although no one could ever know it in advance, including myself.

What I can say, is that the frantic search for something to do or become, the inability to stay still and reflect on our habitual patterns, and the certainty that happiness is the future somewhere are all signs of inner conflict and dissatisfaction. It's an amazing and beautiful thing to have the energy and intention to become better people, and cultivate habits that will benefit others and ourselves. But the main difference between this kind of behavior and the kind mentioned above is that we are, at some level, already satisfied and joyful prior to achieving the goal we have in mind. In other words, the seed of our goal has been growing within us because we are watering it every day. If our goal is to be happy and peaceful, our intentions, thoughts, and actions on a day-to-day basis must be in alignment with our goal, even if only to a small degree. We are mindful and motivated to be a work-in-progress—happy and peaceful people in the now. What gets us in trouble every time is the illusion that happiness and peace will come in the future if we work hard in the now, to get things we don't have and to become people we aren't yet.

There is such a perception in the fitness world. Most of us engage in exercise and healthy eating for the wrong reasons. A quote from Kabir, the Indian mystic poet and saint, says, "If a mirror ever makes you sad, you should know that it doesn't know you."

It might come as a surprise to some of you, as it did for me, to hear that most of our so-called "healthy" habits are actually escapisms from deep-seated, negative mental states. Cultivating habits that distract us from understanding the real sources of our pain can be very attractive to some of us. Discovering the real sources of our suffering takes not only hard work, but a genuine intention to end suffering. Not all of us are ready to let go of what propels us into habitual ways of thinking and living. We have the tendency to hold on to anything that is familiar and makes us feel comfortable, even when in actuality we are extremely uncomfortable. Of course, it's not that we like to suffer—we'd just rather maintain our conventional way of thinking, which accepts unnecessary suffering as something normal.

It is true that we are conditioned to experience pain in this life; however, most of our suffering is self-created. An example of this is how convinced we are that happiness will come someday with hard work, even if the hard work makes us unhappy every day before we get to our goal. What we don't realize is that suffering now and expecting happiness in the future is like running a marathon to have a guilt-free moment of enjoyment with delicious, high-calorie foods. How many marathons can we run in this lifetime? And how healthy is it to run marathons anyway?

For many years, fitness was my marathon habit disguised as a "healthy" behavior.

MORE THAN WE CAN "WORK OUT" TO BE

Besides training my own body for years, eating healthily, training others, hosting groups, and participating in fitness competitions, I looked for happiness in my family, in friendships, in romantic relationships, in the arts (dancing, singing, painting), in teaching English, and in meditation—I even had a guru. This is compelling evidence of how most of us believe we don't have enough, or are not enough, to be happy in the present moment. With this in mind, think of how peaceful you are when you aren't looking for something to happen in the now, expecting something to happen in the future, or lingering in the past. As you can see, it is only when the rational mind can't make sense of peace, interpreting it as a waste of time, that we continue our relentless search for happiness and meaning.

As an illustration of this, I will share a brief period in my life when I took a break from going to the gym and being on a diet. I'd been causing myself pain by forcing my body to exercise out of pure habit when it needed to rest, and by maintaining a restrictive diet when what I really needed was to feel the pleasure of having chocolate mousse again. As a result of taking time off, I gained a few pounds, but my body felt incredibly good. I had no more soreness or joint pain on top of the emotional distress I suffered from being married to Vicente. I began to feel joy.

In contrast, Vicente became agitated and unhappy. He'd often ask me sadly why I couldn't live a normal life and go back to the person I had been. There was an odd feeling every time we were close together—I felt he was in mourning around me, as if somebody had passed away. The person I was before, that "normal" one he referred to, was an unhappy, anxious, insecure, fearful woman with whom he had had a depressing relationship. In my present state, when I was feeling better and calmer, my husband couldn't relate to me anymore. Note how we get used to others' old selves and miss them when they are gone, even when there was nothing good or wise about them. To believe we are unchangeable is what gives continuity to suffering.

Although this was a truth I could see at the time, before giving any serious thought to changing my situation and divorcing my husband, I felt enormous pressure to go back to the gym and diet again. Not even meditation could save me from these habitual tendencies. Exercise and healthy eating habits were the "positive" distractions that kept me from examining my inner soreness. I had been a "practical" depressed woman for many years.

We can't underestimate the power of habits. They can seduce us into a life of compounded and continuous suffering, while the mind gives us all sorts of "healthy" excuses to perpetuate the cycle. In my case, my mind would say there were worse things than being unhappy; at least I had the "healthy" habits of exercising and eating clean. In actuality, this was a pattern of physical self-abuse disguised as healthy habits.

Then there's our delight, as a society, in the idea of being busy. We spend most of our waking hours thinking about how we can achieve, reach, get, use, grow, and create. In making these self-realization plans, we don't leave enough space to feel our own existence and the joy already present in our hearts. When I fell into depression, I realized it was not for lack of temporary happiness in external things. It was a call for a much deeper understanding about life, especially my own life, in which I realized that addressing the causes of our unhappiness can prevent unnecessary suffering.

For years, exercise was my drug of choice to ease the excruciating pain brought on by lack of self-love and fear of not being accepted by others. For you, it might be something else; but the suffering is the same. It is that dissatisfaction we feel with the present moment—that I don't want to be here. We'd rather be in our memories of the past, or dreaming about a better future. Worse yet, when we finally feel the present moment is perfect, we sabotage it out of fear of losing it. We are propelled into action based on old habits, hoping to secure a future that can give us brief moments of bliss that will soon be washed away by fear again. The cycle of suffering seems endless.

The amazing news is, our suffering is not endless. In fact, we can end it by realizing we are participating in a cycle of negativity and habitual tendencies carried on in our daily lives. For those of us who have had enough of the cycle created by our own negative states of mind, the end can come sooner. We simply stop doing what makes us suffer, or shift our perception of reality into one that accepts the situation we are in if we can't change it at the moment. This doesn't have to be a difficult thing to do for those with the genuine desire to end suffering. For example, if you eat something that makes you sick, you stop eating it. If you have a tendency to get angry at your partner, drop the anger or drop your partner. The compulsion to do something out of habit, even when it's causing us pain, is not an impulse that comes from our positive state of mind.

There are studies that show exercise has a beneficial impact on depression, and I don't doubt it. It has also been said that mindful meditation is an excellent way to calm our minds. While exercise and meditation can be tools for improving memory and health, my years of experience fighting depression (not that I knew I was depressed) with exercise made my problem worse. I became addicted to fitness as a way to relieve emotional distress while keeping the cause of my suffering unchanged. The fear of changing my situation was based in false beliefs and insecurities that had no basis in my actual ability to live happily on my own. In many ways, I was still a hurt child who needed attention; having others around to smile and praise my body meant they cared for or loved me, which developed into a dangerous and warped dependency on romantic relationships. The list of bad relationships in my life only grew with every toned part of my body. I was twice unhappily married for a total of almost two decades, trapped in a painful cycle where I went from one relationship to another looking for love and acceptance in someone else's heart. It didn't take long to realize I could not find what I was looking for in my marriages, so fitness became my way of coping with the pain of that realization, too.

At best, this strategy redirected the focus of my life to the pursuit of a fit body, which gave me a temporary "feel good" sensation and a false sense of purpose. It soothed the symptoms of what would soon return as major depression.

While I was still coping with mild depression, in a constant state of inner conflict and silenced agony, I used to spend lots of time at the gym, not only working out but also socializing. I'd come up with new healthy meals so I could invite friends to my house. But when I was alone, I wondered why I couldn't smile to myself, why I still felt ashamed of being me, why I was so lonely even though I had a long list of friends and a maxed-out number of connections on Facebook. I questioned the reasons all my marriages and other romantic relationships failed. I didn't know what to do about my dissatisfaction with my new career, even though I was apparently experiencing the most successful time of my life.

You know the feeling you have when something is wrong, and you know blaming others or the world won't make it right? I knew this, but I had no idea how to make real changes within myself toward a genuinely happy life. Talking to friends about this feeling and hearing their breezy reactions made me feel worse. Those around me believed I had everything and that I was whining. Although my intention was to be loving and kind, I found myself obsessing over physical fitness and attractiveness. The depressed identity is hard to break free from, but I find the "fit person" identity even tougher to let go of. This is because it is perceived as a positive, healthy habit, and everyone around us reinforces that notion.

As a general rule, exercise is a healthy practice, especially when it becomes an enjoyable addition to our already happy lives rather than a distraction for our unhappy minds. There was a natural fitness competitor I knew who ended up hospitalized as a psychiatric patient after training and competing for many years. Afterward, she stopped going to the gym and competing altogether. I remember looking at pictures of her online. It was hard to recognize her at first; she had a peaceful smile on her face. In all the time I'd known her, I had never seen her smile.

For the most part, we spend our lives trying not to disappoint others by maintaining the role model identity we've created. Being healthy and fit was my way of showing strength and inspiring others. What I didn't know was that the real meaning of strength was to be kind to myself. I had to be able to do that first, before I would ever be able to be kind to others.

WHAT STRENGTH IS NOT

The word "strong" is often associated with physical strength or brave actions. But to me, real strength lies in finding the truth about what causes us to suffer, especially the kind of suffering that is avoidable—like keeping a job we dislike to maintain a good reputation with our family and friends. How can we possibly be kind to others when we aren't with ourselves? Having work that provides financial support for ourselves and our families is important and meaningful when we are also able to provide ourselves with happiness. In other words, when we are satisfied with our way of making money, it results in treating others with kindness. Do you realize how the belief that we are strong and inspiring for working endless hours to help others turns into resentment? I've seen this over and over amongst my family and friends. My mother worked really hard to provide us with food, shelter, and clothes, but she wasn't happy. This resulted in uncontrollable bursts of anger and aggression from her when we made a mistake as little as dropping a spoon. If this is altruism, it's a form of "unkind altruism" at best.

In one of my vigorous training days, I was climbing a high set of steps outdoors. Many people passed me, including an overweight mother who was having a hard time carrying her baby down the steps in her stroller. I passed her at least three times as she struggled to descend, but it never occurred to me to help her. All I could think was that by passing her as fast as I could, as many times as possible, I would inspire her to engage in exercise so she could lose weight and become a stronger and healthier mother. Later that day while walking home, a couple who passed me said that I was strong and courageous for climbing those high steps. Had I actually been strong and courageous, enough to listen to my spiritual heart, I would have stopped to help the mother and her baby. Instead of inspiring her to be fit, more importantly, I'd have motivated her to be kind to strangers.

We often don't question the motivations behind our actions until we get badly hurt by trying to balance our need to be seen as good with our deep desire to simply be happy and kind. My twenty-year relationship with the world of fitness was my journey between the heart and the mind, the past and the future, and love and hate. This struggle would eventually expand into a spiritual awareness that discredited the illusion of joy which existed apart from the present moment created by our intention and motivations. I profoundly believe that embracing reality as it is and practicing kindness toward ourselves and others are the foundations to a truly healthy and happy life. There is no exercise program or diet plan for a kind heart; in fact, the opposite is true—the kinder we are, the happier and healthier we become.

How many of us are ready to be strong and courageous enough to live authentic lives guided by the heart? A simple intention such as not lying, when we practice it every day, can create a deep and positive chain of changes in our lives.

With this understanding of being kind to ourselves, we also begin making changes in the way we treat our bodies. Have you noticed how easy it is for us to show compassion toward animals and children? I feel we do this because they seem innocent and vulnerable. When it comes to our bodies, we seem to have a different view. But isn't the body innocent too, apart from our minds saying it isn't? To blame the body for being the cause of suffering is like blaming dogs for barking, birds for flying, small children for crying, or lions for hunting.

From a deeper, spiritual perspective, the body didn't ask to be born, we did (that is, our minds did). Think about the Buddha's teachings for a moment. He said the mind is everything; what we think, we become. The body, then, is simply the manifestation of the mind to fulfill its desires and carry on its aversions. Therefore, the mind is responsible for all the harm done to the body, beginning with its creation. How often we defy the simple logic of cause and effect and hurt the body because of our negative habits of thinking! We smoke, overeat, and engage in sexual misconduct and substance abuse, among other self-destructive behaviors.

Why do you think most of us engage in unhealthy activities even when we clearly see what lies ahead for us? Negative thinking habits were at play, long before we realized we were in this new body. This is easy to see in the fitness domain; we work out hard, usually hurting the body, so we can have the ice cream we must have.

Perhaps to help improve this basic mind–body disconnect, we can begin by treating our bodies with kindness. If the Buddha's perspective that thoughts create our reality makes sense to you, even the smallest change in your habitual ways of thinking can greatly affect your life.

When I spent a few days treating my body as if it was an innocent pet, my mind began to direct my actions toward favoring my body's health over habitual-negative tendencies. Since most of us love and treat our pets well, this perspective can begin to shed our resistance to loving our bodies, accepting them as they are, and treating them with kindness and respect. It's shocking to observe that even the conventional and apparently great relationship we develop with our bodies to keep them in shape and healthy turns out to be an abusive agreement. It certainly was for me, with strenuous exercising and restrictive dieting. I was both ashamed of my body and unkind to it.

The following story illustrates this mind–body disconnect. The mother in this piece represents a mind distracted by the habit of gossiping, and her son represents the innocent body.

A mother is taking a walk around her neighborhood with a friend. They are engaged in an interesting conversation. The mother's four-year-old son is inside the stroller she's pushing.

The two women gossip about TV stars and their friends' private lives. It's early in the morning, and the neighborhood they live in is in the center of a big city. There are many intersections and cars on the roads. The women constantly have to stand and wait to cross at stop signs and stoplights.

At one point on their walk, their conversation gets so interesting that they don't realize the stoplight is red. They cross the street when they shouldn't, and fail to watch for traffic. When they reach the other side of the street, the boy starts to cry and moves about uncomfortably in the stroller.

A few minutes pass before the mother gives him her attention. The conversation between the women has reached its best part: the TV star they're talking about has taken a lover, and his wife has found out about it.

When the woman finally asks her son why he is fussing so loudly and unhappily, he says, "The light was red and you didn't see it. You don't love me!"

Horrified, the mother realizes what she has done.

* * * *

Note how the mother is so engaged with her thoughts that she forgets she has a body. Think of how often we don't smell the scent of our shower soap; we don't feel the texture of the toothpaste in our mouths; we don't see or hear the bird singing at our window. We have no idea what our breakfast tasted like minutes after we ate it. This is because we often live in our thoughts of the past and future. Our bodies are actually much more interested in the present moment than our minds are. The body will let you know right away when it is uncomfortable or unwell. Even when the mind knows it is causing these problems, it often tries to deny or ignore its self-sabotaging effects.

Also think of how we run around doing things all day. Our minds don't stop thinking of strategies for achieving our goals. We strive to succeed financially, intellectually, and emotionally—we want to win, to master, to be the best. We want to become somebody others will respect—never mind self-respect. Exercise is often one more item on our to-do list. We want to be in our best physical shape, or oftentimes, we are actually afraid of losing our health over this restless race to sign up for things. I've heard innumerable times about the idea of "balance." It never made sense to me. What are we trying to balance? A stressful lifestyle with happiness and serenity? The notion of balance, in my view, is much like getting sick every time we eat fish but still including fish in our diets so we don't just eat red meat and chicken. I've often had the feeling that what we refer to as "balance" is actually the cycle of engaging in stress-relief methods to counteract our stress-causing habits and behaviors.

Under these circumstances, it can become harder and harder to understand intellectually that we can experience constant happiness and serenity, though this is indeed an accessible reality in our minds. As I mentioned before, to access this precious way of living, we must be genuinely tired of the cycle of suffering we are causing in our own lives.

From the window of the subway one day, I saw huge words splashed bold and bright across two advertisements. First, there was a set of three words displayed on an advertising panel for a fitness facility: "Strive—Achieve—Grow." Ironically, this ad was above a deli that had the words "Beer—Soda—Lotto" written on its red awning. This comical juxtaposition reminded me of a darker belief system many people keep in their lives. The effort to achieve and become, if it does not bring joy in itself, falls short of our true goals of happiness and satisfaction. The excitement, anxiety, or euphoria that comes from working to achieve external things often intersects with the need to numb an ever-present fear that our desires and efforts might not be achieved or will expire. This is when drugs, alcohol, exercise, overeating, the lotto, or other distractions become part of our lives.

Chapter 5

Fitness Before Spirituality

THE BODYBUILDER OR THE ARTIST?

I was at the gym. It was late, about eight-thirty. I was stretching after having just finished my workout. I sat down on the mat for a moment, looking around. I was not looking for anything or anyone specifically. I was thinking about what I would have for dinner when I got home.

My eyes spotted Santiago, a young bodybuilder in his early thirties. We had spoken before about fitness competitions while I was preparing for a show. He used to be a competitor, too. He came over with a half-smile on his face. I got up to greet him.

"How are you feeling, Santiago?" I asked.

He lowered his headphones. "Just starting my workout, feeling okay." He swung his arms as if dancing to the hip-hop song he still heard in his head. "But I'm ready for a badass workout tonight. My new routine is called Beast Mode."

He was moving and looking around. His eyes were out of focus. He was wired with wild energy. It didn't feel natural to me, but I smiled at him.

"What do you mean by 'feeling okay'?"

"I am good, doing good," he said in a mildly melancholic voice, looking around.

I was deep into Greek philosophy at the time, so I asked him, "If you knew you would die a month from today, what would you change about your life?"

Surprised but curious, he turned his head and looked at me for moment. Then he said, "Wow, that's a good question, I never thought about that." He paused for a moment, thinking. There was no looking around anymore. He was focused, looking up to the ceiling. He said, "I would go back to drawing. I used to draw when I was younger, but I had to stop to work at a finance office to make money." He looked at me for a second to see if I was listening to him.

He continued, "It has been ten years now. I hate my job. That's why I come here to make my body sweat. It relieves my stress, anger, and anxiety. If I knew I would die soon, I would quit my job and spend the rest of my days around my family, drawing." He said all this while looking up. His body language was calmer, as if he could picture this kind of life.

"Do you know when you are going to die?"

"No, I don't know, and I don't want to know." He squeezed his eyebrows together, unhappy with my question.

"Santiago, you should stay around your family more and go back to drawing."

He raised his shoulders and released them with a loud sigh, turned around, and went back to his hip-hop moves to start his beast-mode workout.

A few weeks after our conversation, one of Santiago's friends came to me.

"Hey, Valeria. Do you know what happened to Santiago?"

"No," I said, a bit worried. His friend didn't look cheerful. "What happened?"

"He died three days ago."

"Oh my God! How?" I said.

"Drug overdose."

I had a long conversation with Santiago's friend. I asked him the same question about how he would respond if he knew he'd die soon. He said he believed in God, and if his death was God's wish, he would be at peace with it. I like what he said, although only the moment of death can confirm his faith. To be in a peaceful state of mind before and while we are dying is, to me, the most beautiful statement of pure love.

However, the best answer to the "dying soon" question I've heard came from a woman in her eighties. She said she would continue living her life the same way. Knowing that her physical death was approaching wouldn't change a thing. She was spiritually alive, and she knew in her heart that the spirit never dies.

BODY-MIND MISFIT—
FITNESS COMPETITION EXPERIENCE

Participating in a fitness competition was not a decision I made with my heart. After my second divorce, I upped my fitness program a notch to deal with my insecurities and disappointments. This new, extra-strength numbing drug translated into extreme workouts and a very restricted diet. I quickly began to look like a fitness competitor after the change.

Everyone praised me at the gym and asked when and where I would be competing. I had no idea what they were talking about. (I also found it interesting that muscular men were never asked these questions, but a muscular woman was assumed to be preparing for a special show or sport.) I guess it didn't occur to them that pain also builds muscles. Perhaps this is a hidden secret of the fitness industry; it certainly was for me.

It didn't take long for me to grow curious and begin looking into fitness competitions. I read everything about them—their processes, federations, dates, costs, locations, and coaches. The competitions themselves didn't interest me, but the idea that other people would admire me more and might change their own lives because of me was enticing. I also had a hidden agenda, which was to impress Ray.

I registered for the next show, which was in four months, and hired a coach. I refined my diet and exercise routine. It was painful and expensive. I maxed out all my credit cards. I felt horrible, but I was looking more and more "shredded," as they say.

I went from 125 pounds to 113 in four weeks.

During my preparation, I ate pre-planned meals every day, almost always the same foods. These meals were high in protein and low in carbohydrates. Even though at times I just needed a slice of bread with peanut butter to feel better, I trained myself to ignore that need.

I exercised seven days a week, despite my body's painful complaints. I believed that being in the best shape of my life was more important than listening to my body. Although I didn't expect to win the show, I was convinced that just participating in it would be worth all the physical pain, mental depletion, and disharmony I felt with my heart. My mind was in control of the situation. Its justifications went from impressing everyone around me, particularly Ray, with whom I was infatuated at the time, to making more money as a trainer. None of it resonated with my heart.

Other excuses my rational mind gave to continue the physical abuse and obsession were discipline and purpose in life. Being disciplined meant proving myself to others; purpose meant doing whatever it took to get ahead in that reality. There was nothing natural about preparing for the show, nor in the lifestyle I adopted.

Before this experience, I still ate healthily, but I did so only when I felt hungry and I always enjoyed my food. I exercised to relieve emotional distress and to distract myself from pain. When prepping for the competition, I was eating foods I didn't like every three hours when I wasn't hungry. My body became tense, and my mind was confused most of the time. I didn't understand why I was doing it all, yet I justified the experience as necessary. I exercised to follow my training protocol, not to relieve stress, which in turn doubled my emotional pain.

At this time, I was still training many clients every day. I took all the pre-planned meals with me in small containers with lots of ice. I carried heavy bags all day all over Manhattan by train, and ate the cold food whenever I had a break between sessions, sometimes in the restrooms of residential buildings. I did cardio at midday, and after a long day of work, I lifted heavy weights with the help of creatine and BCAA supplements.

Three times a week I met my coach, Lisa, to take body fat measurements, go through some basic poses, and discuss my progress.

Our meetings didn't take long—about thirty to forty-five minutes or so. Most of our communication was done by email, phone, and text. She was a seasoned bodybuilder who had won many competitions in the USA and abroad. Her approval and support were more important to me than her knowledge. Her experience with this industry fascinated me. She mentioned on various occasions how unhealthy this entire fitness competition concept was, that it contributed greatly to eating disorders, physical abuse, and mental confusion. Most of her clients, herself included, had taken all kinds of drugs to look how they were supposed to for these shows and had paid a high price in their overall health. She personally had been battling persistent inflammation for years. Lisa was one more person in the fitness industry addicted to looking good and portraying a positive lifestyle like I was. Even though we sensed the danger of our supposedly healthy habits, we couldn't stop our obsession with seeking gratification from their temporary results.

The strenuous training and restrictive dieting presented below are not a suggestion on my part to any of you; they are only meant to illustrate the extreme protocol competitors go through, especially on show day. This is what an unclear mind can lead us to do. The so-trusted "rational" mind can lead us into action conventionally recognized as brave and inspirational, but there is nothing brave or inspirational about the pursuit of a lean and "ripped" physique when the heart is not happy and kind.

As with all the content in this book, my motivation is to share my experiences and expand your view on both physical and spiritual fitness.

Show-Day Protocol

The menu below is included only to illustrate what my personal journey was like. It is not an approved meal-plan recommendation.

I woke up at seven in the morning, went to the bathroom, and then to the kitchen to consult my meal plan for the day:

- No fat can be added at the first two meals
- Sip on water only: 1-2 glasses total
- Take dandelion root supplement with every meal
- Water pill after second meal (I didn't take it)
- *Meal Plan*
  - Meal 1: 5 oz white fish or 6 oz egg whites and veggies
  - Meal 2: 5 oz white fish or 6 oz egg whites and veggies
  - Meal 3 (before the show): cheeseburger, fries, and a piece of candy
  - Meal 4: 4 oz of salmon and veggies

* * * *

I had my first meal—no shower because the night before I'd had a bath of airbrush tanning. I had to be very careful not to mess it up or I would look like an unfinished painting. My face was also painted with the brown stuff, but that didn't concern me much. I lived alone and was supposed to eat and drink very little, except for a meal before going on stage.

Everything was ready. The competition suits were ready to go. My food was packaged in a bag full of ice. The show started at nine in the evening. My makeup appointment was at noon and stage rehearsal was at five. They were each at a different location, and there were long breaks in-between. One of my Manhattan clients offered me her apartment to stay in during the break, as it was close to the event theater.

I was nervous and hungry, but unsure which was influencing the other. I'd questioned my decision to get myself into this since the beginning. On competition day, my internal voice grew louder: *What am I doing?* I had no answer apart from, *I am already ready here, don't complain.* I felt confused. I'd never wanted to compete, but I was so committed to the charade that I couldn't go back. It was like wearing a pair of tight and uncomfortable shoes for hours just because I'd paid a lot of money for them and couldn't exchange them.

The cab arrived at my place in Astoria. I went down with all my gear and headed into Manhattan. I arrived at my client's apartment and took all my stuff from the cab; it took two trips to get everything inside. I'm not sure if I said hello to the doorman. My mood was so dark I don't think I would have said hello to myself at that point. I felt a need to get things done quickly, as if that would lessen my pain. It was like walking fast in those tight and uncomfortable shoes, hoping time would pass by quickly, too.

It was still early, ten o'clock, when I arrived at the apartment. Alone, I looked at myself in the mirror. I felt so lonely and empty that I wouldn't have been surprised if it hadn't reflected anything back. I was in the best physical shape of my life. I was ripped—the result of months of self-control and hard work—but instead of feeling proud of myself, I felt ashamed and sad.

I was glad when it was time to go. My thoughts needed a distraction. I took a cab to the makeup site. When the elevator door opened, I heard all the women talking about how they wanted their makeup done. Some were eating their green beans, some were fixing their hair, some were complaining. None of them seemed to be enjoying anything.

My first thought was, *I don't belong here.* I wanted to retreat into the elevator and forget about the whole thing. Of course, I didn't do that; I did exactly what all the other women were doing. The feeling of being unable to stay and unable to leave struck me again. I was stuck in another situation in which I could only push through to the other side and hope I learned a lesson in the process. Everyone was in a bad mood, except the receptionist who took my payment. Fortunately for me, when I deal with painful situations, I let joy take over. In such moments, I am carried away by gratitude for being alive and around others. My heart fills with the hope that we can still connect despite our trying situation.

The connections I was hoping to make with the women there didn't happen, not even with the makeup artist and her assistant.

The competitors were all anxious or angry about something: their eyelashes didn't fit well; their makeup wasn't enough; their hair didn't suit them. They were all living in the future, for the time when the announcer would call their names. Everyone in that room was clinging to the moment in which they would hold a trophy, filled with happiness they hoped would last forever.

I was grateful that the time went by fast. My makeup was done in thirty minutes, and then I was back on the streets looking for a cab. I returned to the apartment to spend some more time with my melancholy. I put on my first outfit for the show, then put on a long robe to cover it up. I was in high heels, and though I'd taken posing classes in preparation, I was still uncomfortable wearing them.

When it was time to go, I managed to drag all my stuff out of the apartment, through the lobby, and to the curb in my high heels. There were a lot of things I needed to carry. I stood there, missing my sneakers like a mother misses her child on the first day of school.

It was four o'clock in the afternoon on a Saturday, and Broadway was crowded.

People passed by me with looks of incredulity or curiosity, as if they had never seen a muscular woman in heels—well, they probably hadn't, at least not at that time of day. There was a hot dog stand close to me. For a moment, I forgot about the taxi. I couldn't believe it, but I wanted one of those hot dogs. Hell, I could have eaten twenty of them. I didn't realize it at the time, but my intense "fitness" regime was every bit as unhealthy as that whole cart of hot dogs.

I was uncomfortable wearing shoes I couldn't take off, hungry when I couldn't eat, thirsty but couldn't drink, and anxious but unable to take a deep breath. My coach said I needed to squeeze my belly at all times and look the happiest I'd ever been in my life. What a painful lie.

It was something that shouldn't have been hard for someone like me, who had lived to please others, but this was an extreme version of faking perfection for validation. Did the other competitors feel like me? I wondered how professional models did their work. Was all the fame and money they had worth going through these moments? It was hard to believe anyone would say yes.

I never thought I would win the show. Going through the process and getting as far as I had was already my prize—a prize that didn't mean anything more than impressing my friends, family, and my new date. I had invited everyone, of course.

A cab pulled up outside of my client's apartment building. I carefully put everything in the trunk; finally, I was on my way to the venue. Before saying hello, the driver asked me, "Are you a model?"

"No. I will be posing for a fitness show," I replied.

"You look great," he said with a big smile. I thanked him, and he watched me with a smile through the rearview mirror. It was like hearing a joke I didn't understand while everyone laughed around me.

The car stopped outside the theater. The smiling driver helped me take my stuff from the trunk. Inside, I dragged everything through the hall and followed the arrows backstage. I found a place to park my heavy bags and sat down in an isolated corner. I wished I'd brought a book with me—not that I would have been able to concentrate enough to read, but at least I would have looked less awkward. The whole time, I felt like I didn't know what I was doing.

The women around me were in worse moods than they had been at the makeup sitting. I tried to talk to some of them, but they were brief conversations.

"Hi. My name is Valeria. What's yours?"

"Hi, Lisa. Excuse me; I need to fix my makeup." Lisa turned and walked away. After the same thing happened more than three times, I decided to stop introducing myself.

I tried to get comfortable in my tight corner. I missed my moments alone in my client's apartment; at least there I could look sad. At the show, I needed to smile and look like I was having the best time of my life.

A woman came in, screaming, "Attention, attention, everyone!" It was the stage coordinator. "You all need to be ready to rehearse in ten minutes."

I stayed where I was, feeling ready to go. I wasn't going to attempt to talk to anyone anymore. Everyone began to rush to get ready for the rehearsal. The place was packed with huge themewear costumes, shoes, bags, food, and girls moving around. Some fixed their makeup; some ate; others got dressed and made noise without really talking to each other. The stage coordinator came back again and screamed, "Get in line. Get in line, everyone!"

We all started to line up. There were two lines. I got in behind a tall blonde woman. The coordinator looked at me from a foot away and pointed at me. "Hey, you in pink. What is your category?"

"Fitness Model," I said.

"You are in the wrong line." She mumbled something else I couldn't hear.

We moved along, heading to the stage, when the girl behind me said, "You need to put your number on."

I thanked her, got out of the line, and went straight to my bag to pin the round metal frame with my competitor number on my suit. I rushed to get into one of the lines again. Half the girls were already on stage walking around. They were doing what the coordinator said.

I was about to walk on stage when the coordinator screamed again, "Hey, you in pink. You're in the wrong line again! What a stupid girl!"

Everyone was looking at me. I tried to hide behind the women around me, feeling like I'd made the worst mistake ever. My body began to shake with fear and embarrassment. I wanted to cry, but I couldn't let tears fall. Tears were used to being hostages inside my body in these types of moments. Besides, they would ruin my tanning and makeup. I managed to compose myself.

I went through the rehearsal and tried not to look anyone in the eye while still smiling. I tried extra hard not to make any mistakes and to stay in my line like an obedient cow—no, even worse, a cow in high heels. The whole event had turned into a real-life nightmare. I counted the seconds till I could be free of the nightmare, wanting desperately to awaken in my bed. But it was only six-thirty; there were still two and a half hours to go.

I didn't make any other mistakes during the rehearsal. At the end, I was still confused about which line belonged to which category, and I couldn't ask anyone, but I managed to not get yelled at. During the time between the end of the rehearsal and the beginning of the show, I pretended to be busy, either by straightening the three-hundred plus feathers of my large theme-wear costume, or by staying as long as I could in the restroom to hide from everyone. It was another two and a half hours of silent despair.

When the show started at nine p.m., I took a quick look at the audience to gauge how many of my friends and the other twenty-some people I invited had come. I didn't see anyone. People who weren't competing were not allowed backstage. I figured my friends were there somewhere, or perhaps they were late or still outside.

I got in line—the right line. When the announcer called my name, I forgot all about my physical and emotional discomfort. I walked on that stage thinking to myself, *I am confident in who I am, and who I am knows no fear.*

I couldn't see anyone in the audience; the lights were too bright. As I started to pose, I heard people screaming my name. I was nervous about the idea that people were watching every step I made and judging me, but I was confident that I was there representing much more than a body. These thoughts made me relax a bit and remember what I had learned from my posing coach. Her biggest advice was to squeeze my abs, advice I totally forgot for the most part. The scariest moment on stage was the "comparison line." This was when we all lined up to face the judges and audience, and the presenter called us out, one by one, to turn left, right, back, and so on. We were all so nervous that it was hard to hear what the presenter was asking us to do, which was humiliating. Think about a dog when it hears a strange sound; it gives a fixed and confused look directed at no one, then goes back to what it was doing. It's funny now when I think about it, but it was awful to be in a situation like that as a human being before a large audience, judges, and cameras. During my entire posing presentation on that stage, I felt like I had survived a plane crash. I was still figuring out where I was and what had happened as I tried to project gratitude for being alive.

I remember the moment the announcer crooned, "And first place goes to... Valeeeeeeria!"

I was not expecting to place at all, so winning was an enormous surprise to me. I quickly walked to the front of the stage, managing to squeeze my theme-wear between the other two competitors in the way. I stood there because I'd heard my name, but I still couldn't believe I'd won first place in my first fitness competition—not just in one category, but in both categories I'd registered for. My smile was wide as the cameraman took pictures. I smiled out of the confidence I had in my heart that I was much more than just that body.

There was no prize for winning.

After the show, I realized that from the dozens of people I had invited, including my coach, only one person had come to see me—my ex-husband, Vicente. The Brazilian woman who had designed my theme-wear was there too, but not to support me; she came to see her work on stage. As she later quipped, "You only won the show because of my work."

Vicente took me out for dinner. For the next three hours, his familiar presence comforted me. Although he delighted himself in an endless monologue about all the beautiful women there, I was just glad to be out of that nightmare. Vicente regaled me with his womanizing feats and unfiltered recollections of how he'd wanted to jump on stage to kiss the petite brunette in red. It seemed he had a different reason for being there than to cheer me up.

As I crawled into bed, I realized how alone I was in the reality I had created. Over the following days, my obsession with food also became obvious, but by that point there was nothing I could do about it. By starving my body for months, I had created an unhealthy and uncontrollable relationship with food that I was powerless to stop. I would eat a whole jar of peanut butter in a day, but avoid the bread because I was afraid of the calories. As punishment for my gluttony, I would run for hours despite my aching hips and knees.

Nothing about the experience resonated with my heart, but it made me understand why it had happened. To know the light, I had to first meet the dark. And dark it was during this period of my life. Depression hit a few months after the show.

PART THREE

FROM DEPRESSION
TO JOY

Chapter 6

Walking the 'Fit for Joy' Path

A MYSTERIOUS FRIEND

It was a calm, late afternoon in October. I was walking next to a "friend" who'd surprised me with her visit. She caught me leaving the train station on my way home.

"Oh, it's you," I said. "I never thought we would meet one day like this. What a surprise."

"You called me," she said.

"I did?" Strange—I didn't remember calling her. I knew I hadn't been able to sleep the night before. That's all I remembered.

We walked slowly along the streets of Astoria, New York. The ten blocks to my place meant we would have a lot of time to talk. I'd been training clients for hours, and my friend was talking nonstop, pelting me with questions. I was wearing my trainer uniform and my favorite orange sneakers. My friend was wearing my thoughts. We were talking about my life.

"Why are you so sad?" she asked.

"It's a long story." I sighed. "But to sum it up, I feel my life has no meaning and no purpose."

"Why do you say that? You are a role model for so many people. You are healthy, attractive, and in top shape. You just won first place in your first competition! What are you talking about?

"You make great money training clients. You live alone in a cozy apartment in New York. You have lots of friends—well, not anyone like me, of course!" She coughed and added, "You just ended your bad relationship—you know, the one that drained you for years. I know that the guy you met recently, the one you thought was 'the one,' just broke up with you, but you have so many other things to be happy about, Valeria."

She said all the things I didn't want to hear. I knew most of the things she said were supposed to make me feel joyful and whole, but they didn't. I told her, "I don't know what to do. I feel as though I don't belong to my own life." My energy dipped, and my gaze fell to the sidewalk.

"Oh, come on. Cheer up! Let's have a glass of wine or eat some cookies. You'll feel better," she said, laughing.

"Why are you laughing? I'm hurting and I don't understand why. It's not funny," I said to her. I was losing patience with our talk and her laughter.

"Okay, okay, I get it. It seems all you need now is a new man. You will be fine when you fall in love again." She laughed even louder.

The streets were quiet. We passed by a Mediterranean store on the corner where the old, friendly Greek owner sat out front. Normally, he would say hello to me, but today his head was down and he was mumbling to himself, perhaps about to fall asleep. I was glad—I was in no mood to chat, and I was sure he wouldn't want to meet my friend.

"You are so quiet. What do you think about my last suggestion?" My friend persisted as we walked past the store.

"I feel I've lived my whole life on a stage, performing all kinds of roles. I never knew how to perform the role of being myself. I don't know a different way of being," I said to her, hoping she would get me this time.

"I understand exactly what you are saying," she said, looking at me. I was so glad to hear that. But then she continued, "Of all your friends, I am the only one who knows who you are, and I am going to tell you the truth: The lights are off."

"I'm sorry—what did you say?" I asked her, puzzled. I had no idea what she was talking about, but I was curious to hear what she was going to say next. She looked at me seriously, straight into my eyes. We stopped walking. She braced herself on the sidewalk and faced me.

"Valeria, you have no stage to perform on anymore. There are no more roles to play. You have no audience. The lights are off."

That phrase again: The lights are off. I shook my head, speechless, just looking at her.

"What do you mean by all this? Especially the 'lights are off' thing. You're scaring me," I said. What happened next frightened me to my bones.

I imagined we were standing in the middle of a stage with the lights off. My friend disappeared. I stood alone in the dark. I could hear only my anxious breathing.

Moments later, everything around me disappeared. I had no idea where I was or what I was doing there. I felt as though I had lost my mind, but I had no other choice but to stand there, quiet, hoping my friend would say something.

And she did.

"I have a question, Miss Fitness. What role will you play on this stage if the lights go on again?"

I had no idea what she was talking about. I stood there in silence, afraid of the dark, just wanting her voice to continue.

"As I expected, you don't know anything about the 'stage' you are on. Here's the deal: I will turn on the lights for a moment. You are going to have just enough illumination to get off this stage and step onto another one." She didn't sound like she was kidding, and I wondered if maybe I really had lost my mind.

"Go on—as soon as you start to walk I will turn the lights on again," she said.

It sounded like an order. I had to do what she told me. What else could I do? With my first steps, I could see again. My heart raced.

I was back on the street of my neighborhood. What a relief! I was still confused about what had just happened. Everything looked brighter than I had ever seen it. It felt like I was walking those streets for the first time. It was a feeling I'd never had before, of experiencing something new even though nothing had changed. I looked around for my friend. She was gone.

What about the other stage she'd mentioned? *I don't see it*, I thought to myself.

It was all too strange for me. I was glad to be back on Astoria's streets, and to feel normal again.

I walked home. When I got there, the first thing I did, as usual, was turn on my computer. I was not looking for anything, really. There was a feeling of joy in my heart, mixed with a sense of purpose.

My inbox was open. It had many unread messages. The top one said:

> Subject: From Your Mysterious Friend!
>
> Dear Valeria,
>   We had a useful conversation today. I hope I could help.
>   There is one more thing I forgot to mention: Find out who you are so you don't have to play roles anymore.
>   —Death

This passage is meant to illustrate my state of mind during a period of major depression. For about two weeks, while I presented a fit and healthy body and experienced my most successful moments as a professional, I had lost interest in life.

What seemed to be a rational conversation with myself while having suicidal thoughts was actually my mind trying to understand the reasons I felt the way I did; it was a state I'd never been in before.

Many of these thoughts simply insisted I had no reason to live anymore, and at the same time, others would explain the reason for that; they'd blame me for pretending to be positive and strong when I was weak and filled with resentment about my past.

Although the hopeless thoughts left me apathetic, with no energy to try to numb them with exercise, food, or talking to friends, the other thoughts were giving me hope. They were enough to assure me that I wouldn't end my own life; my only choice was to wade through the feelings moment by moment and try to understand what they wanted to tell me. This is obviously not the best way or time to learn about what your life is about—but as those of us who have been depressed know, this state of mind can emerge anytime.

While energy-draining thoughts can scare us because of their seeming aloofness toward life, I feel we should pay most of our attention, if possible, to the energized thoughts that pass through our minds, especially if there is anger behind them. This, for me, was crucial. The strongest thoughts I had were those that brought back my past and all my resentment toward my family, particularly my mother.

After days of dwelling on my detached feelings and memories of the past, there was a moment of silent melancholy before a question that would change everything: "What would you do if you were still alive?" In other words, if I could change something in my life before I (physically) died, what changes would I make? I knew the answer well. I'd listen to my heart.

A feeling of profound joy and peace overtook me in that moment. I smiled and smiled to myself—in awe of this wonderful state within me that had been hidden for so long.

From that day on, I looked for ways in my life that I could express the voice of the heart over the noise of the mind. Besides being kind and gentle toward myself and those who had hurt me in the past, my heart found other ways to express itself, one of which was the idea of writing this book.

IS THERE A STOIC HEART?

Besides a major shift in perspective, significant outer changes might also be a requirement when following the path of the heart. This was so in my case.

As you know, by this point, all my disappointing experiences as a personal trainer and fitness competitor led me into inner conflict, followed by a period of depression, which brought to the surface the realization that love is what life is all about; it also pointed out the negative feelings I had been holding onto.

This promise to listen to my heart constituted an irrevocable shift, and I knew I couldn't go back to training private clients or working out the way I had before. Although training and eating a healthy diet for most of my life hadn't granted me happiness and peace, nor saved me from having a chat with death, I also knew I could still help others and myself by bringing matters of the heart into the world of conventional fitness. I decided to give it a try, right where I was in New York City.

In my online research about depression, I came across ancient Greek philosophy and Stoicism. Stoicism has been associated with CBT (cognitive behavioral therapy) for a while. It was founded in Athens, Greece, in the early 3rd century BC, and practiced by Epictetus, Seneca, and Marcus Aurelius. The philosophy announces that wisdom can be transmuted into happiness when applied in our lives through cultivating our rational view of life. It teaches that we don't control, and cannot depend on, external events, and the cause of most of our suffering is our false beliefs in relation to the nature of things. It spoke to me, as I believed I was an emotionally strong person because of my ability to deal with challenges and my resilience. My mind was transfixed.

I had the idea that by becoming a Stoic fitness trainer, I'd be able to help others see that all the negativity in our lives is rooted in false beliefs. I then added to that philosophy that once we understood this, as long as the heart was the master of our lives, it would be fit, happy, and loving.

Motivated by the desire to help others and myself, Stoicism became my model for keeping negative thoughts away. It was a way to listen to my heart while keeping my role as a fitness professional and writing my book.

Since New Yorkers are inclined to get involved in intellectual activities, I stopped training most of my one-on-one clients and began a group program called "Strength and Wisdom," which later became "Fitness and Philosophy." It combined exercise, nutrition, philosophical discussion, and meditation. I opened a Meetup account and advertised the meeting online and offline.

The gatherings went well; around twelve to fifteen people showed up to our very first meeting. They were men and women between twenty-five and fifty-years-old interested in exercise, deep conversation, and meditation. We met at a fitness studio initially, and later outdoors in the parks. I made matcha green tea for everyone after the exercise portion of the class, and we talked over a healthy snack. We practiced meditation at the end of the session. After each session, a few members would stay around to talk more intimately about their lives, and sometimes they'd come to my house for dinner. These people turned out to be beautiful human beings already on a spiritual path, and we became good friends.

At the same time, I had the feeling that engaging in exercise, long philosophical conversations, and meeting new people was not helping anyone with the matters of the heart, but only taking our precious moments together deeper into the games of the mind. Although the idea was interesting and positive, in practice, it was not even getting basic understandings across, such as the importance of healthy relationships both with others and ourselves. I realized that our group members were actually more attracted to the idea of meeting new people than working on themselves.

The premise of these gatherings was to create awareness about the link between self-knowledge and happiness, which begins with identifying our negative habitual tendencies. And how crucial this was (and is!) in building healthy relationships, especially with others. Some of us bring new people into our old lives (or our old ideas of ourselves), which, for the most part, are illusory and unhealthy. To me, this was a serious issue, because we tend to rush into all kinds of relationships with selfish desires and needs, turning life into a nightmare for everyone. The group meetings created the opportunity for this to happen before my eyes. I witnessed a few members openly share their problems with all kinds of addictions and then ask each other out.

It was time to find another way to help others and myself establish a deeper faith in our own hearts. I ended the group meetings to focus on finishing the book.

What I didn't know was that my *Fit for Joy: The Healing Power of Being You* journey had just begun.

THE BLANK PAGE AFTER THE WORDS

My heart was no longer beating to New York City's rhythm, and with the end of the group meetings, I was left with a book to finish. Although I was a personal trainer promoting well-being, my being wasn't well at all with my current situation. I needed a quiet place to write and be alone for a while. I set up a crowdfunding campaign for the book and contacted a number of friends who lived outside New York and abroad. At the time, I also had an idea for a fitness center project that would be called "The Fitness of the Heart."

Within two weeks, a delightful proposal came from my French friend Nathalie. She suggested I stay in her house in Créteil, a quiet suburb of Paris, where I'd be surrounded by pristine lakes, tall pine trees, and lovely white swans. I couldn't be happier!

A few months later, the book campaign was funded thanks to all of my dear friends and family. I was ready to establish my newly found inner peace in Paris. Nevertheless, what I didn't know—but would soon learn—was that quietude and nature are not the same as the joy that resides in our hearts. Even when inner peace is present, major physical and mental activity can still be part of our daily lives. I believe these activities to be linked to our aspiration to generate happiness for others and ourselves. A good example, in my case, was writing this book. There was an enthusiastic and highly energized motivation to finish it and to find a publisher, which took almost two years, discipline, and lots of hard work, besides going beyond the fear of being criticized or disliked.

The peaceful-active state I discovered throughout this period was interesting. While my mind was busy with thoughts about the next chapter, story, or paragraph for the book, I was actively living in the present moment, as if the past didn't exist and the future didn't matter, although they did. I was simply a woman with a body that loved carbs and sweets, and I had a mind that manifested all kinds of thoughts and feelings: sadness, anger, lust, happiness, fear, and desire. Yet somehow I didn't feel as if I was just body and mind. It was like finding a bigger and more expansive part of me that embraced it all without feeling constricted by whatever I chose to engage with. I was the thinking mind (aspirations and motivations to act) and the body (craving carbs, sweets, and also exercising; joy was being externally stimulated all the time). However, I could witness the gap between these states and find a peacefulness being there, too.

How did this understanding, or rather experience, come about? I had felt it for a moment during depression, when I finally overcame it, but I couldn't put it into words then, let alone sustain it for long. In France, it opened up. It became an ongoing feeling, and freedom is the best word to describe it.

I believe that being alone in an unfamiliar environment can reveal the unknown "self" that renews the familiar one. I believe that feelings are responses to the natural relationship we have with our environment and experiences. We are all unique and respond differently to what surrounds us.

In New York, I was caught up in being the personal trainer to clients whom I thought didn't embody the true meaning of health, when in fact, I also didn't. I was a disappointed fitness competitor who abused her body for months preparing for competitions. I was the twice-divorced woman with a traumatic past who was struggling to forget my pain and forgive. All along, deep inside, I was yearning for gentleness and peace that only my heart knew well while the mind tried and failed to conceptualize it.

In Paris, I was simply a human being in a quiet place doing what I needed to do without playing a specific role. I was writing, but I was not "the writer," and I was training, but I was not "the trainer." Do you see the difference?

I ate when I was hungry; there was no judgment about what I ate because the super-fit competitor wasn't there. I was mentally and physically busy, but I felt like a tree that remains calm and still throughout the changing seasons.

If we can learn how to create space for action without losing touch with the serenity in our hearts, we can live with joy all the time. It was clear to me that we become stressed, anxious, and depressed because we have limited our minds to act and react according to our psychological, emotional, and physical aspects only. Think of it this way: when you are in your heart, you can be overloaded with thoughts and physical activities, and your peaceful state won't change as long as you are not attached to the identity of the "person" you normally are—the person with specific tendencies, habits, likes, and dislikes. Rather, you become an open being who embraces it all, the good and the bad. By accepting what comes, within and outside of us, we make good and bad disappear. What remains is life the way it is.

What's amazing is that we can live like that starting right now, by recognizing that we are actually serene beings living a human life with endless potential for joy in each and every moment. We can do this without disassociating from our physical bodies and our psychological reality. Most of us suffer because we hold on to who we think we are. Try to reflect on this for a moment; it takes a lot of thinking and work to be a consistent and "solid" person. In a way, we're simply recreating the past in the present moment, over and over again, when life is movement, flow, and change.

Our journey to joy and away from unnecessary suffering begins when we start to experience ourselves as beings who constantly refresh their thoughts and renew their beliefs. When we get to the point where we no longer feel the need to ask about the meaning of life, how it all came to be, and what will happen when we die, we've started to truly live in the center of our hearts. When we tap into the heart's reality, we transform our lives into a joyous adventure.

While the goal of my trip to Paris was to finish writing the book, I now realize that my unconscious mind brought me there so I could begin the process of learning more about the person I thought myself to be while introducing the new one I never knew existed. In a sense, we need to keep getting rid of our old selves in order to renew our lives with the happy and peaceful version of ourselves.

Let us be writers of stories that become blank pages after they have been told.

When we understand that the essence of our nature is not the thinking mind, but rather an infinite space and timeless quality inside of us, joy arises. We become free of unnecessary pain. Once we establish ourselves in that place of joy, everything can be seen as a lesson of love.

Peace and joy don't come from a healthy body or a rational mind that dwells in thoughts and memories; they come from a much subtler reality called the spiritual heart. There is much to say about the unkind reality created by the rational mind—especially in our cultural structures—which ignores the heart's reality. The rational mind is a great servant that becomes dangerous when turned into a master—the heart is the only master that can create a kind and healthy reality. This is so easy to demonstrate. Think of the way you feel when you fall in love with someone, or after you've spent time with puppies. Now, think about living in this state of mind most of the time.

The limited physical reality most of us live in is a painful one. We entertain ourselves with achievements, pleasures, and excitements, but also suffer dissatisfaction and disappointments, confusion, and lack of wisdom in the face of sickness and death. It's hardly fun to dwell in the past, worry about the future, and constantly fight to maintain what we think we have or acquire what we believe we lack. This kind of worldly life is an endless marathon toward suffering, but it can be replaced with joy when you access the truth inside your own heart.

When we know there's a lot more to us than our bodies and thinking minds but we don't know how to access that deeper part, we end up struggling between the two. This limbo can be interesting, especially because it can teach us to have compassion for our own bodies. However, the paradox is that giving attention to thoughts about fitness and health can lead us to believe that we are physical beings whose psychological needs must be met to feel good or to be whole. At this level, we are not living a spiritual existence yet.

The negative aspect of our mind can have such a powerful pull that it can make us believe there is only one reality, called negativism. So long as we are convinced that we are only our physical bodies and our thoughts, there can be no joy. Living under the constant influence of our negative thoughts means that peace and happiness will always be temporary. In contrast, when we know that we are also spiritual beings, our happiness becomes less and less dependent on thoughts relating to our external reality, where most of our negative feelings come from. Note how quickly we become angry, sad, or fearful when we think of someone we don't like or a painful situation we went through.

The levels of reality as I understand them are thus: at one level, we are physical bodies (genetic pre-dispositions and cultural habits); at another, we are emotions (psychological traumas, needs and wants, and the yearning for happiness and peace); and at another level of reality, which I call the "heart," resides peace, love, kindness, and all the feelings that bring us together. I contend that this is the reality in which we know we are "fit for joy"—perfect beings!

Because we are mostly aware of our physical and negative psychological realities, our minds dwell on countless desires to compensate for the confusion of not knowing the source of our suffering. Fitness then has great appeal—don't we all want to have a fit, healthy, and attractive body? How many of us are satisfied with our bodies? Who can we refer to who's not afraid of losing his or her physical attractiveness and health? Wouldn't it be a much different reality if we trusted our heart, which show us every moment that happiness and perfection exist only here and now?

The French priest and philosopher Pierre Teilhard de Chardin wisely said, "We are not human beings having a spiritual experience; we are spiritual beings having a human experience." This is something most of us intuitively know.

In Brazil, an attractive body is worshipped as if it were a god. I was not only taught to strive for physical beauty, but also to be obedient, to serve, and to smile. It took years of inner conflict for me to accept my imperfect body and find my way back to an intuitive faith in my heart, a heart that had always known my true identity as a spiritual being.

When I was very young, perhaps eight or nine, I had a compelling experience to which I responded as a "soul." Looking at myself in the mirror one day, I had the spontaneous thought, *Oh, I am back in a girl's body.* No more thoughts followed for the next few minutes. I stayed there, contemplating my body as a new vehicle for my unfolding life. There were no other thoughts judging the initial one. I remember that for a while, I saw my life as a rebirthed soul. This was not merely a belief about myself; I perceived others as souls, too.

Looking back on my difficult upbringing, I can see why I thought as much. I endured such sadness, pain, and confusion that part of me never lived entirely in that reality. I knew somehow that all my troubles were only as real as everyone around me thought they were. My environment was heavy with anxiety, fear, and cruelty, which affected my happiness. I didn't always handle everything well and calmly, but when I was alone, I'd feel the still presence of perfect joy, love, and serenity.

My spiritual experience as a child was a powerful reflection of the truth about different kinds of realities. Age, however, brought doubts, identification with the physical body, and psychological imprints that would make me forget this spiritual awareness. Every time I thought about this early experience, my mind dismissed it as false or insignificant. I created all sorts of explanations for the event.

We have the tendency to dismiss what we can't understand with our rational minds, even if it is the most beautiful experience. It was by dismissing the truth in my heart that my pursuit of a fit and healthy body began. After investing so many years in physical and psychological health, I finally realized that true health comes from knowing the depths of our own hearts and the nature of life. With this knowledge, all my external searches for happiness and peace ended, and a joyful celebration began. We don't need to find the way back home when we realize that leaving home was only a dream.

As I already noted, fear and insecurity can turn physical fitness into an addiction. While most of us consider the pursuit of physical fitness to be a great habit, for me, it was a painful cycle disguised as a healthy practice. The more unsatisfied I was with myself, the more strenuous, restrictive, and obsessive my exercise and diet became. Looking back, it's clear to see that dissatisfaction was what drove me to dedicate more than twenty years of my life to fitness. I strongly believe that the reason fitness and fit people are so popular is because most of us are attracted to the idea of having a "healthy distraction" for our inner conflicts. Although it is true that exercise and physical attractiveness can improve our overall health and lift our self-esteem, to use these methods to hide our pain can also result in increased, unnecessary suffering. I don't know anything healthier than having the courage to delve deeper into our own hearts for answers.

Chapter 7

Integrating Fitness
and Spirituality

THE HEALING POWER OF BEING YOU

With spiritual understanding comes wisdom. It's time to take care of our bodies with intelligence and kindness. The name I give to this marvelous combination is "The Healing Power of Being You."

When we get to know how our minds work in relation to exercise, our methods to stay physically healthy become very different. We now acknowledge how easy it is to exercise for the wrong reasons—that is, for its powerful effects as a numbing drug for emotional pain—instead of for its natural benefits, such as promotion of general health, boosting our self-esteem, increasing our feel-good moments, promoting better brain function, and improving our physical appearance and strength, among others.

Be aware that fitness can still become a dangerous addiction, even after hard spiritual work. I caught myself overtraining after spending days in meditation. We can never underestimate our habitual tendencies. Although spiritual knowledge, coupled with the guidance of our own hearts, can prevent exercise from becoming an unhealthy practice, it is my belief that we still need to surround ourselves with those who are on the path of "true health" to create the environment that will allow us to practice our virtues consistently.

With spiritual understanding, we will recognize that the heart is a far better master for our lives than a state of mind that dwells in the future and past, causing us to suffer in the present moment. A good example of this is my entire fitness history, as you now know. I'd engage in exercise either to ease emotional pain rooted in past traumas, or to look good and healthy enough to disguise my pain in the future. The end result was more pain, since I didn't enjoy my workouts in the present moment. At certain points, I was dwelling so much in my mind that I could hardly feel the physical pain I was causing my body.

Once we've done the work of considering these two important points, we will become much more aware of our bodies and mental vulnerabilities, too. We then begin practicing the "Fitness of The Heart," treating our bodies with kindness and gentleness. There's no more running with knee and hip pain because we must keep some sort of role-model label intact. I am not saying we should give up running altogether. Instead of denying our fragilities (in this case our need to keep running, which can be connected to the psychological need to feel good with the help of exercise), we embrace this need with intelligence and kindness. It's kind of like our desire for sweet foods: because of its undeniable effect of making us feel good, once a day we decide to have a piece of chocolate. Note that having a piece of chocolate to satiate your cravings, especially if you choose the darkest version available, like me, is very different from having a whole bar of white chocolate plus a large ice cream cup mixed with chocolate cookies!

In my case—having endured chronic stress in response to emotional tension for an extended period of time—exercise has indeed proven to be a wonderful medicine. As John J. Ratey states in his book, *The Revolutionary New Science of Exercise and the Brain*:

> At every level, from the microcellular to the psychological, exercise not only wards off the ill effects of chronic stress; it can also reverse them. Studies show that

if researchers exercise rats that have been chronically stressed, that activity makes the hippocampus grow back to its pre-shriveled state. The mechanisms by which exercise changes how we think and feel are so much more effective than donuts, medicines, and wine. When you say you feel less stressed out after you go for a swim, or even a fast walk, you are. (Ratey, John J., and Eric Hagerman. *Spark: The Revolutionary New Science of Exercise and the Brain.* Little, Brown & Company, 2013.)

So, we can keep working on our physical and physiological health, not as a method to achieve happiness, but as a way to keep it on the surface in our day-to-day lives. There will be a remarkable shift in your habits as you progress and deepen your spiritual understanding. For instance, my tendencies to eat large-size meals and practice high-impact exercises didn't go away with my spiritual understanding. But as a consequence of my new and deeper views about life, my kindness increased, turning me into a vegetarian. As my mind became more serene, I also began to choose places to live that were closer to nature. As a result, I now eat large-size salads, and my workouts have turned into long, enjoyable walks around and in nature.

FIT, HAPPY, AND KIND

If, like me, you can't stay away from physical activities, integrating fitness and spirituality is essential. How many of us have struggled to answer how to take good care of our bodies, without falling for preconceptions of physical attractiveness and health? The answer is both very simple and highly complex and paradoxical at the same time. However, the closer we live to our spiritual hearts, the less we tend to engage in physical activities as purely beautifying or self-cherishing methods, even when these activities promote good-looking bodies, health, and higher self-esteems. At this point, we are wiser, joyful, and peaceful enough to work on our bodies, thus we hang around longer to support others through our virtues.

I find the most enjoyable way to unite body and mind during an exercise session is to make the activity spiritual—to bring the heart into it. What is interesting about this is that our "souls" will ask again for the experience, allowing mind and body to benefit greatly.

Although physical health is an important asset, the reasons we engage in exercise can still become unhealthy. Being mindful about these motivations for hitting the gym or engaging in any physical activity is helpful if you are seeking spiritual growth and self-knowledge. Be on the lookout for these unhealthy motivations to exercise:

- The need to be thin to feel good every day.
- Pressure to look good and lean to attract a new partner or to please an existing one.
- Feelings of insecurity about a specific body part.
- Fear of not being loved by others if you are out of shape.
- Guilt for not exercising every day or more often.
- To release stress caused by a changeable situation.
- To release anger.
- To show off, get attention, compete, or provoke envy in others.
- To fight or to intimidate others.
- Out of pure habit without enjoyment.
- Shame.
- Pressure to be a role model in your family, work, town, or society.

These are just a few examples. Keep in mind that behind all these reasons to work out, there is fear, and it is fear that makes them unhealthy.

In contrast, when you've found joy in your own heart, you'll have a much different experience when exercising. There should be a body-mind connection where you find yourself in the moment. There is enjoyment, no fear, and less concern with your physical health; you are simply respecting the natural law of cause and effect. You experience satisfaction before, during, and after your exercise sessions, and feel anxiety-free about your next workout.

Exercise is a great habit to cultivate, but should not be an obsession. There should be no expectations to get specific results apart from improving your overall health. There should be no guilt when you don't exercise. The main motivation should be to live longer and be physically healthy so you can do more spiritual work on yourself and help others to do the same.

My advice is that you find your own unique way to connect with that deep feeling of love while moving your body. We have all heard of yoga, tai chi, and Pilates as workouts that connect the mind, body, and soul. I feel that any exercise can be transformed into an act of meditation or a powerful spiritual experience, even an ordinary, daily walk. Here are some ideas:

- Choose any exercise you feel you might enjoy or already have experience with.

- Exercise in nature. Feeling the divine forces around your body relaxes the mind and prepares it to feel the divine presence. We are all wired to reconnect with pure love and kindness. Trees, rivers, flowers, rocks—all these mindless beings are divine reminders of your true essence.

- If you are in your house or in a closed space, listen to love- and kindness-evoking songs or mantras. This is a beautiful way to enter a timeless and spaceless vibration. You will find that the physical effort involved in the exercise becomes less noticeable.

- Drink a cup or two of matcha green tea. This tea is beneficial for your health, offers an instant sense of clarity and focus, and increases energy and well-being. It has been used by Zen Buddhists for centuries in their spiritual practices.

- Listen to speakers whose presence and words open your heart to love and kindness.

⟩ Light a candle or incense.

⟩ While it is good to exercise every day, don't force your body into it.

As for food, diet plans and nutritional advice are important and helpful. However, true living is an ever-changing flow of experiences which calls for constant self-knowledge, openness, and self-love.

Because many of our eating habits are based on immediate self-gratification, diet plans and nutritional advice become ineffective in the long run. I witnessed many of my clients embrace clean diets in the pursuit of fitness and health, only to return to their usual eating patterns soon afterward. They were looking for a quick fix to their unhappy states of mind. Be on the lookout for anything you do that has a "have to do" factor. This means your mind is much more in control of your life than your heart is.

The way I see it, many food cravings (though certainly not all of them) are directly connected to anxiety and fear. This may be because the mind has associated happiness with pleasure, but since pleasure and pain are closely related, suffering paradoxically becomes a tasty experience. The body, on the other hand, craves food and sex for self-preservation and perpetuation, not pleasure. It's interesting to notice that only the heart, which is rooted in love and kindness, has no cravings that can cause us suffering. The heart cares for our being as a whole; it also cares for others, happily and healthily embracing everything as a big family.

It's not hard to tell when there is a body-mind disharmony. We can recognize this through simple and real experiences like eating or drinking something that makes us sick. We then know that eating certain foods harms our bodies, so we don't do it again. In the same way, it isn't unreasonable to assume that if we take the law of cause and effect into consideration, for example, killing animals to feed ourselves for pleasure, rather than necessity, will have a negative consequence in our lives in one way or another. Many of us experience feelings of compassion when preparing or eating animal flesh, and some even reject meat at childhood. I am not trying to be righteous by saying this. My observation is that most of our suffering is caused by lack of awareness of natural laws. Sometimes it's simply a matter of giving thought to our behaviors that seem natural when, in fact, they're only habitual tendencies that perpetuate our pain and that of others.

I remember when I first decided to stop eating animals because I was unhappy with my life and myself. It was midmorning, and I was cutting a whole chicken apart when I suddenly felt that I had no right to eat that animal's body. I had an interesting thought: My life was too purposeless and unhappy to sacrifice a chicken's body to feed my own.

It may not make sense to you now, but it made so much sense to me then that I became a vegetarian from that day on. For about five years, I was a fake vegetarian. I say "fake" because I still craved meat, but pretended I didn't. I felt morally entitled to criticize those who ate meat. I wanted everyone else to be vegetarians, too. I argued about animal rights and became defensive when criticized. Self-pity had turned me vegetarian, but it didn't teach me anything about self-love. I was like one of those angry peace activists.

In light of this thought, I feel we only start living an authentic reality of love and kindness once we've become that reality within ourselves. Then our lives, actions, and behaviors will reflect our inner state. The concept of becoming spiritual doesn't appeal to me as much as becoming aware of our non-spiritual selves. Not eating animals only because it's a "spiritual thing to do" when we still desire to eat meat is like saying we are kind people while killing someone. We must remember that our thoughts and actions will align themselves perfectly and gradually with whatever stage we are in during our spiritual journey, even if we are not ready to accept ourselves at that stage. By pretending to be holy, we will only invite more suffering and confusion into our lives.

There is a paradoxical perception that we should do the "right thing," even if it feels forced, so we change our minds. As everyone is different, it may eventually work for some of us; however, in my experience, by forcing myself to be good I was actually causing further pain to others and myself. In the example above, I was not eating meat but I was still craving it, while getting angry at those who were not vegetarians. Instead, we must get to know and be friends with the unkind people we seem to be, until we recognize the loving people we really are.

Note how so many of us lose weight only to gain it all back shortly after. We can say that we were not prepared to be thin. Likewise, some of us aren't ready to be kind and gentle toward animals because we don't yet see the link between our suffering and the suffering we inflict on other sentient beings. It is only by living as spiritual beings in physical bodies that we'll be able to understand how interconnected everything and everyone is. Knowing this, we won't be able to hurt others. It's like one hand cutting the other; it wouldn't make sense to us.

I've stopped eating meat again, but this time it's different—I don't crave it anymore. There are no more conscious thoughts involved when I go out grocery shopping. Something in me is attracted to vegetables, fruits, and grains, and it feels natural. I have no negative feelings toward those who eat meat or disgust toward slaughterhouses and seeing animal parts, although I feel incredible kindness for those beings that are losing their lives in such a way. On the contrary, if I still craved meat, I would assume that my spiritual understanding wasn't yet deep enough to become a vegetarian. Becoming a vegetarian is certainly better for our health; it is also a beautiful act of kindness when there is no strong belief hiding behind it, especially the belief that you must do it to be spiritual. You are a vegetarian simply because you harbor no energized thoughts that propel you to eat meat.

In the event that vegetables, fruits, grains, nuts, and legumes begin to look more attractive to you than meat does—and if they resonate more with the truths in your heart—a sequence of other changes may also occur. You may stop drinking coffee, alcohol, smoking, or eating peanut butter. It happened to me. Though I continue to have an a good relationship with food in the sense that it makes me more joyful. The best recipe I know for a healthy life is to keep the heart open and kind.

Chapter 8

Voice of the Heart

LISTENING TO THE HEART OR THE HABITUAL SELF?

It was a sunny afternoon. I was leaning against a wooden fence watching swans and ducks swim in the lake. I was at the top of a bridge looking down at the water. A wonderful feeling of peace and joy filled my heart. My breathing deepened and my body relaxed.

I could stay here all day, I said to myself. Then a question came to mind. *Why does watching these birds make me feel so peaceful and happy?*

I had no answer for a few moments as I kept watching the birds swim. Then came an answer: It was because they were free. It was a sunny day, and they were swimming in an open lake in whatever direction they chose to go.

A mother with her child passed me. The child laughed, pointing at the birds. They distracted me for a moment, but it didn't take long for another thought to occur. This time, as gracefully as the birds swimming in the water, I thought, *Oh, I know. It's the beautiful pattern they leave in the water as they move with the freedom that comes from being themselves.*

* * * *

Isn't that what happens to us when we think and act from our hearts? There is no fear to love or be loved, and with this freedom comes the joy from the positive impact we make on other people's lives. Make no mistake: happiness and peace belong to an open heart.

How do you know you are listening to your heart and not your habitual self?

We can't stop the flow of thoughts. They will always polarize our minds. However, the nature of our thoughts and the degree to which they command our attention can change radically depending on our lifestyle and spiritual practice. Here is my list of eleven signs that your heart is becoming the master over your mind:

- **Less judgment.** There is kindness in the way we respond to our imperfections or to the mistakes we make. This extends to how we see and treat others as well. Being our own best friend is how we become someone else's.

- **Helping others.** There is a great feeling of joy and fulfillment when we can benefit others.

- **In the moment.** Whatever we do feels special. There is a magic quality to this moment. We are here and now fully embracing life as it comes.

- **Serenity.** In the heart's reality there is no time, space, or fear. Anxiety is linked to fearful thoughts about our current life. Peacefulness is connected to trusting in the natural flow of changes.

- **Let it be simple.** Because the heart knows life is essentially about love and kindness, it rejoices in simple things. There is no reason to complicate what is meant to be simple.

- **Silence.** The heart is in touch with different levels of reality; it enjoys silence from our minds. Those who listen to the heart treasure quietude.

- **Joy.** Passion and excitement are replaced by joy. Passion is often linked to desires and pursuits of temporary achievements, while joy is rooted in renewal, love, and acceptance of what is.

- **Nature.** Feeling at home in nature is a sign that the heart is in control, at least in that moment. Nature, especially places that are surrounded by trees, mountains, and rivers, bring out the stillness in us.

- **Interconnectedness.** We are more in touch with that "feeling" that connects us to everything.

- **Playfulness.** Why take life too seriously when its nature is change and transformation?

- **Quick to forgive.** Forgiveness is the mother of peace of mind and the biggest contributor to happiness.

Another important sign that we are listening to the heart and trusting it to guide us is the refreshment that occurs in our thoughts: we begin to experience life with wonder. Things seem new, even when they are not. When we start seeing reality for what it is through the lens of an open heart, the feeling of renewal and joy is ever present. Take, for example, a painful past, or anything that you label as hurtful, as a lesson of love. It can take a while to come to this deep kind of seeing, but it can happen. I confidently say this because it happened to me. It's the reason I wrote this book.

To start listening to our hearts (the pure, loving, and kind part of the mind), it's important to quiet the judgmental, unkind, and negative parts of it. The less attention and reaction we give to our negative thoughts, the more in touch we will be with our intuitive wisdom. Think of the voice of your heart as the anticipatory feeling you have when you know a decision will bring you happiness and peace—like marrying someone you love, quitting a stressful job, or moving closer to nature—except that true voice of your spiritual heart brings joy and peace exactly as and where you are. The feeling of joy is unconditional; it doesn't rely on anything from the outside. It's a feeling of freedom, of being happy for no reason.

If you observe, you will notice how incredibly bound to the external world our happiness and peace are. If I ask you to think of a moment when you were happy for no apparent reason, how many moments would you describe? Think of helping a stranger in need without a thought of getting anything in return, not even a thank you note. We know how happy we feel when we help others because of all the praise we get or the money we make. But only unconditional joy, a state of being that the heart knows well, can trigger kindness in us toward others that, as a consequence, makes us feel happy and peaceful for no apparent reason.

When we are in the "heart state of mind," there is no loneliness, sadness, or desire to use others for our own benefit. In this state, our decisions are not based on how much happiness we can get from external conditions, because we have become happiness ourselves! We've become amazing human beings who can only emanate kindness and gentleness, from our thoughts to our feelings to our actions.

FORGIVENESS AND COMPASSION

I have met many kinds of people—religious, spiritual, philosophical, psychologically-minded, young and old—who assured me that forgiveness is necessary for a happy life. I heard what they were saying, but it never resonated with the deeper truth in my heart. To me, when we understand that we are all prone to making mistakes, the idea of forgiving someone is not as compelling as treating those who have "wronged" us with compassion and kindness. Think of how many times in the past we were unkind to others and ourselves; if we are honest, we'll admit that we were unable to act differently. To forgive implies that someone outside ourselves has power over our emotions, or that we have power over theirs. How about offering true forgiveness? This is what I call being compassionate, through nurturing a mental state that believes everything is interconnected and nothing happens by chance. Those who are compassionate understand the causes of their own pain and how unnecessary suffering can be avoided. Such understanding drives a person to be kind and loving toward everyone, including people who have hurt them. This attitude is beyond forgiveness.

I am not implying that we should welcome abuse and pain from people who can't yet be kind and loving. It's actually considered a sign of wisdom to try to avoid getting hurt by others. Another sign of wisdom is to not respond with anger and feelings of revenge when others hurt us. If we can't avoid being hurt, instead of welcoming thoughts of anger and revenge, we should do what we can to prevent it from happening again. If necessary or relevant, we may call the police or even imprison those who have hurt us; however, we should not dwell on negative thoughts for years, months, weeks, or days—not even hours. This might be a spiritually advanced level for most of us, but it has been said that one way to tell how involved we are spiritually is to observe how long we spend dwelling on negative thoughts after a painful event.

It took a long time for me to understand the causes of my own suffering and begin my journey toward the end of cyclic negativity. I call it the path of the heart—a path that has been guiding me to real, positive change ever since I took the first step.

My experiences have taught me that most unnecessary suffering is directly linked to our dislikes. We hold on to hostility and resistance toward others, especially those who have hurt us. These feelings propel us into a cycle of suffering that can seem endless.

I recoiled from my mother's anger and anxiety; I detested my father's distant behavior, especially when he drank; I resented my sister's passive aggressiveness and claims to victimhood. But what glares back at me today is how I continued to seek out people with those same traits long after I had left my family. Some will attribute this to textbook psychological patterns of child abuse, but I prefer the Buddhist understanding of the mind, which lucidly explains the trajectory of karma and cause and effect. For me, habitual negative thinking was not a pattern of suffering that would end with therapy sessions (though therapy has been a healthy and helpful step at other points in my life).

For years I struggled to forgive my mother for how she expressed anger when I was growing up. It was a tough joy gate to go through. Imagine a narrow opening through which you can feel immense happiness shimmering on the other side, but to enter you've got to leave behind all the weight of resentment you carry. The joy gate is narrow for a reason. The lighter you become as you shed your inner negativity, the quicker you can pass through it.

It took a genuine desire for me to be free from the prison of my own mind and its tendency to create unnecessary unhappiness. It was crucial to embrace the view that everything is interconnected. In spirituality, this means that any thought of separation is an illusion. For example, judgmental thoughts toward oneself or others feed into very real consequences of anxiety, fear, depression, and discontentment. Take note of your feelings after having any negative thought, and you'll find this to be so.

However, the natural state of our minds houses virtuous thoughts, feelings, and actions, such as love, kindness, compassion, patience, generosity, and courage. These feelings align with the truth of interconnectivity—the truth of our existence according to Buddha.

The Buddha also taught that we are born to families and environments that align with the thoughts and actions we demonstrated in our previous lives. Consider it this way: the greater our dislikes in this life, the more we will suffer, not only here and now, but as long as our minds manifest them into being. Simply put, our negativity or positivity chooses the condition of our next rebirth.

I strongly believe that our negative thoughts from past lives, fueled by untamed energy, are responsible for our suffering in the beginning of this life. Notice how powerful and energized anger is. According to Buddha, the very possession of a human body is evidence of our negative karma. In Buddhist teachings, only the highest spiritual beings who have purified their thoughts and actions can choose the condition of their next rebirth.

I hope this resonates with you as it does for me, because it is this recognition and understanding that guided me to positive life changes beyond imagining. Thus, the journey to happiness and peace begins with the thoughts we are cultivating in this very moment.

I wrote the story of my early life almost two years before writing the book you are reading. In these early pages, I was still stubbornly telling myself that I didn't deserve what had happened to me. I was innocent, the good child. This kind of negative reinforcement of perceived victimhood allowed my mind to build a painful, cyclic reality for me and those around me. The mind could not conceive then what it is aware of now: that I was the cause of my own pain and all the suffering to follow.

Accepting this can have profound effects on our lives. Think about going from dissatisfaction to joy. This is the kind of radical change that a shift in perspective can result in. To me, the aim to achieve such change is worthy even if it takes a whole lifetime. Otherwise, what was the point of our suffering in the past?

The Buddha gave us a very clear teaching about the nature of the mind: Thoughts create everything. I understand this to mean that we created the circumstances of our own existence long before we were born into this life, though most of us don't remember the continuous painful cycle we are in. In my case, I hurt my parents in my past lives. Therefore, it is because of cause and effect, and not as a punishment, that my parents hurt me in this lifetime. With this spiritual view in mind, love, empathy, and compassion can arise, even toward those who have hurt us.

In nature, there is no phenomenon that occurs without cause. The cause may not be possible to trace yet. Our scientific methods may not be able to track backwards through space and time to find the connection between a tree and its origin; however, a tree does not simply exist because it was planted by someone in this lifetime. What about the origin of the seeds and roots that came before it? What about the ones before those? We could go on and on for eons. Buddhism explains that the mind has no beginning or ending. "Beginnings" and "endings" become irrelevant points when we learn to examine the evolution of our minds and how our past selves relate perfectly to our lives in the present.

The core argument of this book has been that we can shift our mind from states of anger, fear, and pain, to states of serenity, happiness, and love. Although this change might be gradual and take a long time for some, the very fact that you are reading these words could trigger major changes in your life—the result of cultivating a realistic mind view that is free of self-deception.

In contrast, expecting fast and easy major changes is a sign of an unrealistic mind view. We've been practicing negativity to perfection for innumerable lifetimes. Even if you don't believe in rebirth and reincarnation, consider this lifetime. Think of moments when you've lapsed into negativity, even dedicated yourself to it. It's a long list, is it not? These spiritual teachings can change our lives for the better, and it matters that we start the work in our own minds now so that one day we can end this cycle of suffering.

Considering these points, we can say that the quicker we can forgive and be joyful again, the more it demonstrates our ability to free ourselves from suffering. This is precisely the reason that having compassion for those who act from their negative states of mind is so crucial for our own happiness.

It took me a while to see the difference between forgiving and being compassionate. But over time, I began to see a pattern. Have you ever had the feeling that your life is going around in circles? That your experiences, especially the negative ones, seem to be programmed into loop mode? One example is the tendency for people whom we wish not to see again to keep coming back into our lives in curious ways. We often meet people with similar personality traits as those of our family members—especially those with whom we've had difficult relationships. You might say this is just chance, but I prefer to believe in Buddha's observation of karmic connection. According to his idea, we have all caused our lives to be the way they are—the people we love are our attachments, and the ones we hate represent our aversions. It's considered to be a reflection of our past virtues to be born as a human being, because it means we have a chance to work further on our minds to turn negative thoughts into positive ones.

For this very reason, we keep bumping into the lessons we still need to learn. I began to realize that I couldn't get away from those who had hurt me—or been hurt by me—in the past. My mother was a great example: her presence remained strong in my life through the actions of others I formed relationships with long after I left my family. It's like watching the same movie over and over and not realizing we are doing so.

Therefore, it's important to recognize this pattern and to stop hiding from those whom we need to forgive. I went further. I began to reach out to those who had hurt me with the intention of working on forgiveness—this changed everything. I no longer meet people with my mother's old personality, for example.

Buddha would say that painful events will keep recurring in our lives, and suffering won't cease until we learn our lesson: to be compassionate toward others and ourselves, which will turn us into blissful beings.

Our minds create both good and evil. The moment we realize that we are not our thoughts, we also realize there is no good and evil—only ideas and concepts. This is how the mind works: it discriminates to understand its reality—that which exists. The heart, on the contrary, brings everything together; it throws good and evil into a bowl, and makes both disappear in love.

How can we still suffer or cause suffering when we know life is all about love and compassion? To say this is not possible, or that we don't want to know how to live this way, is to be attached to pain and suffering. And who wants to be attached to pain and suffering? This is how convoluted the ego can make our lives; it dwells in negativity. The truth is so simple that only the heart can bear it.

Since I started listening and living closer to my own heart, I have seen my perception change in unimaginable ways. When we are open and ready to end the cycle of suffering, all will be healed. The pain will dissolve. No suffering can endure compassion. However, this doesn't mean we don't become sad. With spiritual growth, physical and psychological imprints won't disappear altogether; we'll simply become less and less identified with them.

Long before I ever knew of *The Tibetan Book of the Dead*, I had a frightening yet fascinating experience. I was very tired, about to fall asleep, when I had a dream-like vision. All the people I perceived as "bad" for causing physical or psychological pain to "me" appeared as horrible monsters. The only interpretation I could make was that those people were truly bad, so bad that they visited me in the depths of my mind as monsters. I was convinced the vision had come to me to reinforce my beliefs. Years later, while practicing the peaceful and wrathful deities' recitations in *The*

Tibetan Book of the Dead, I recalled the vision and felt an intense tenderness toward those people I thought were bad. For several minutes, I sobbed and sobbed. I felt as if I was dissolving into love. It was the beginning of a much deeper awareness about living a true spiritual life. The feelings I had toward all the people I had judged as bad were the creation of my own mind, for the mind is essentially empty of all negativity. All negative thoughts are creations of the mind, while love, kindness, compassion, and all other virtuous qualities are in sync with a reality that exists beyond the mind. Again and again, we must return to love and use it as our antidote to heal our negative states of mind. The more certain we are that life is love and love is life, the happier, more peaceful, and healthier we become.

What all religious or spiritual teachings try to do is show us this other compassionate reality, a reality that slips past us when we invest our existence in preoccupations with survival, sex, and power. There are many states of our own minds we are not aware of; in a way, we don't know that our minds are creating our reality all the time. Look around your house and note how many things you have created with your mind. It's incredible, isn't it? This is just what's inside of a house. Now think of buildings, cities, cars, planes, computers, atomic bombs, and everything that makes them function. How come a mind that is so powerful in creating things can't create its own permanent state of happiness? The answer is simple: true happiness can't be created by the mind because it doesn't have to; permanent happiness is already the essence of our minds. Of course, this is true only when they are emptied of all negativity. In Buddhism, the word used is "emptiness," which I understand as freeing our minds from the illusion that anything external can provide us with lasting happiness, or that who we are is separate from joy.

I didn't know before that living in a much more positive and blissful state of mind was possible simply by getting rid of the negativities we can clearly perceive, like resentment. If you decide to practice forgiveness, pay attention to your feelings when people you feel resentment toward come to mind. At first, your feelings won't change—but if you have the genuine intention to lessen your own suffering, you'll soon begin to feel warmth toward those you used to feel hostile about. Then you will realize the incredible, untapped power your mind has. We all know that negative feelings are unhealthy, but most of us don't know how compassion can transform pain into joy. It takes sincere intention, practice, and persistence.

To be able to change our minds to the point of seeing our most painful moments as our best teachers is to know grace. We are not our past; rather, we are the joy and freedom for each difficult moment we have overcome with kindness. In this way, how can we not realize how amazing our existence is? Knowing that life and suffering are inseparable allows us to cease our rejection of unavoidable pain, thus opening our hearts to life as it really is.

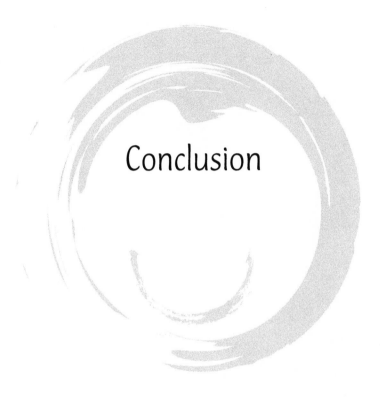

Conclusion

LESSONS LEARNED

Self-Love

From many insights and lessons, I've learned: to have self-love without selfishness; to recognize which behaviors are motivated by love rather than fear; how closely connected my past was to my present; and that love, joy, and peace are at the core of our true nature in relating to others and the world. My new spiritual understanding has not only given deeper meaning to my life, but has also caused external changes I could never have imagined.

MY MOTHER

The woman in the "Porridge" passage was my mother, Dara. Later, when I began to heal, I found ways to heal our past. You would be startled to discover the relationship we have now. It was made possible by my own progress. As part of my new realizations, I was able to affect a reconciliation and achieve true forgiveness and love for my mother. I saw her as the troubled and overwhelmed young woman she had been when she was so impatient with me. She had lost her brother to murder, was mistreated as a child, and endured a marriage strained by the racial tensions of white versus darker-skinned people in Brazil.

I was able to reach out to her—an act of fitness that did not require new muscles, only a fitter heart. She responded in tears, and today she is my best spiritual friend. Even two years ago, I would never have believed this was possible.

In truth, our past is only a story; however, experiences with emotional and physical pain can leave profound negative imprints on our minds. Although I believe my mother didn't know the reason she acted the way she did, my love/fear/hate relationship with her extended into my adulthood. My mind carried on the child's pain that interpreted what had happened to me as "unjust" suffering.

MY FATHER

I thought of my father when I read this story about a weeping fig tree.

There was a houseplant called Batista. He was a talking plant that could only be heard by other plants.

Batista was found in the wild forest and brought to a family's house. From day one, he wished to be reunited with his family in the forest, but he couldn't escape from the house. He was watered and trimmed, and grew his branches only according to the house owner's needs and wants. It made him sad but there was nothing he could do.

Years passed, and Batista started to doubt his origins. He no longer had the desire to reunite with his family. He grew accustomed to the houseplant life. One day, a voice shouting from the window interrupted his nap. "Hello, Batista. Can you hear me?"

It was coming from a tree right outside of the house. Batista was half awake and half asleep when he said to the tree, "Who are you?"

"I am your cousin who was planted outside of this house some time ago. I was not tall enough to see you, but now I am," she said.

"That's nice. Let me go back to my nap."

"No, wait. Talk to me. Are you okay in there?"

It got really quiet for a moment, and then he said, "Do you really want to know?"

"Yes, I do," she said.

"I don't like having my branches and leaves cut off; it hurts. But the smell of delicious food coming from the kitchen makes me forget that I am a plant. I am now part of a new family. Whatever they put in the water gives me sweet dreams. I know I am small, and lonely most days, but who needs freedom and size when you can get struck by lightning out there? At least I am safe in here. I don't envy the sun that shines for you—I know the storm is forming somewhere on the horizon, too. I'd rather live how they want me to live and be secure."

The outdoor tree went silent for a moment, too. Then she said to him, "Batista, I understand your fears, doubts, and confusion. You have believed that you are a house-plant, but you are still a tree—one of us. Even when men create a different destiny for us, we will always be trees. They can cut our branches, cut us to the ground, make us small, water us to live in confined places, burn our trunks, or turn them into furniture and food. It doesn't matter how creative, mad, or controlling they are, they will never make us be anything other than trees. We are free beyond any name or form, and always will be."

Batista listened to her attentively, and then went back to his nap.

FITNESS

I can confidently say from my experience with fitness that the motivation to have a healthy body should not be based on fear, but on love. One of the hardest negative mental habits to break is the constant need for the approval of others. This habit can propel us to physical and emotional abuse, as happened to me, so that we over-train our bodies to be accepted and complimented by others. The more I abused my body at the gym, the more people praised me, and the more I was motivated to keep doing it—to the extent that I even signed up for competition shows. As you can see, this was not any different from a drug addiction. My lack of self-respect and self-love was great enough to keep me open to doing anything that gave me that "approval-acceptance" high.

I now see that my "fit and healthy" lifestyle was made up of a series of these kinds of experiences. I was very disciplined, but it was turning me into the opposite of a loving and happy person. I came to realize that the pursuit of a fit and healthy body could only be a positive thing when we've already recognized our spiritual hearts as perfectly fit to provide us with a life of happiness and peace. In other words, although a fit body can improve our health, earn compliments that boost our self-esteem, and give us a temporary "high" of accomplishment, without a content mind and joyful heart, our happiness won't last long. Our health and feel-good states depend on external conditions and constant hard work, which can propel us into an endless, destructive cycle.

THE PAST

The link between a painful past and fitness became clear to me after a period of major inner turbulence. I knew that most compulsive behaviors have their roots in traumatic experiences, but I never connected my obsession with fitness to lingering inner pain from the past. I believed I was a strong person who had overcome pain because I had a fit and healthy body to prove it, as well as a life that seemed to be driven by and built from authentic, positive, and exciting experiences.

However, the truth was that my fitness habits, to a great extent, were escapism. I rejected examining the reasons I felt forced to work out, even when my body needed a rest. The more I dwelled in my past, the more I needed external relief and heavier doses of distraction. It's interesting to realize now that I was specifically drawn to the kinds of distraction that could create the false idea that I was happy. In truth, suffering was the primary fuel for building my toned muscles and for most of my visits to the gym. Fitness became my numbing drug, and the mirror was a friend who confirmed the illusion that I was well and happy in a fit body. The mirror wasn't a liar, though, it was just the wrong friend to teach or tell me anything about true happiness. How could I ever imagine that my childhood had set me up for this pain and denial, and reflections on it would become the "brutally-honest friend" no one wants to meet? In fact, there was no better way to find the truth I was looking for than to experience the connection of forgiveness and joy.

THE STORIES

I believe our story is part of our spiritual path, and that our spiritual path is inseparable from our story.

During my period of inner conflict as a fitness trainer, I did sense that something was wrong with my thoughts, behavior, and my life in general, but I had no idea that the pressure to be fit was directly linked to an unhealthy desire to please others based on past experiences and conditionings. What keeps us repeating the same mistakes and suffering unnecessarily is precisely our inability to address our negative past as stories. They can help us better our lives if we pay attention to them with courage and kindness. We can learn to perceive all past experiences—without judgment, blame, or guilt—as references for what not to reproduce in the present and future.

DEPRESSION

A few months later, still at the peak of my "new life," the feeling that I couldn't help my clients intensified as my façade of success crumbled. The fitness competition I had won had been an awful experience of self-abuse that made me obsessed with keeping my weight as low as possible. The new guy I'd fallen in love with was my ex-husband in a different body. My emotional life was falling apart.

On a calm day while walking home from the gym, I started having frightening thoughts. I didn't think about ending my life; rather, something deep inside me suggested it was already over. Despite my fit and healthy body, years engaged in the fitness community, and my organic diet, I was severely depressed.

I felt I could not share my condition with anyone. After all, I was a fitness model and a "health" enthusiast. Being perceived as a strong and inspirational person was crucial to helping the people around me become "healthy." Thus, my depression had to remain hidden.

Although I knew my clients were making positive changes in their lives because of me, I intuitively acknowledged that these were not the kinds of changes that pleased the "soul." Pained and lonely, I trusted I would overcome depression and feel "normal" again by spending more time at the gym, coming up with new exercise routines, new healthy and delicious recipes, or buying new gym clothes. But my depression worsened until on a sunny, beautiful day, I felt that I was dead. I couldn't think of anything that made me feel that I deserved to be alive. My past was filled with painful experiences and torturous memories, from childhood abuse, to two divorces, to unreliable friends, to dissatisfying careers. In the darkness of my own mental prison, I asked myself, *What would you do if you were still alive?*

This was the question that changed everything. Before I even thought of an answer, joy washed over me, and immediately I knew that my understanding of life had shifted. I felt like I was free from all the pain. This feeling also announced that happiness and peace had been there in my heart all along. I promised that I would listen to my heart from that day on, starting with forgiving my mother. There would also be no more preoccupation to be fit as a way to be happy. I was, and always had been, fit for joy!

This feeling was so real and strong that all I wanted to do was to share it with others. I wanted to tell everyone that no matter what happened, is happening, or will happen, there is a path to true happiness.

HOPES AND DREAMS

Deluded dreams and unrealistic hopes for the future can have the same effect as real drugs. We all know something is terribly wrong with this frantic search, but because everyone else around us is living in this kind of reality, we get pulled into it too. We start to believe that this is how things should be, that this is what is real and normal. In truth, what is real and normal is to fully live in the present moment.

Consider this: if we can't find happiness and peace in our own hearts in this very moment, doing whatever we are doing, we won't find it anywhere else or at any time in the future. Our hearts know and have known the truth forever.

To strive, achieve, and grow without joy is to live in mediocrity; it is much like the unfulfilling pleasure you experience while having a beer or soda and playing the lotto. Where is the joyful you in this moment?

THE HEART

It's with profound delight that I can say the main message in this book came out of my conviction that we are in physical bodies to realize the joy that already exists in our spiritual hearts.

Fit for Joy connects physical activities with spirituality and enjoyment, and psychological processes with our inner nature, which are our unique ways of seeing the world based on our past experiences. I believe that the heart is the master of our lives, the mind our powerful servant, and the body the bridge between them.

THE PRESENT MOMENT

Happiness and serenity are linked to the present moment, which requires fully appreciating what is happening now, within, and in our environment. Nevertheless, many of us do not achieve this state because we dwell in the past or become preoccupied with living for a "better" future. When we project or stake our happiness on the hypothetical achievement of a future circumstance, we sabotage our ability to be happy in the present, and reinforce a self-destructive mindset that will likely persist into the magical "future" we are hoping for. To release ourselves from this trap, we must shift our perspective toward a spiritual reality that resides in the now with the power to transform pain into joy.

THE JOY

Writing about these life events taught me that everything is connected, and that ignoring what causes us to suffer is the same as losing an incredible chance to free ourselves from pain, thus abandoning the path of happiness. This might sound contradictory; however, I assure you from my own experience that there is nothing like examining the causes of pain and fear to free ourselves from them.

We are not our past, our thoughts, our feelings, our genes, or our futures. So who are we underneath it all? Well, I highly suspect that we are joy—a mixture of peace and happiness! It's my conviction that only the heart can empower us with true forgiveness, joy, and love; with its undeniable healing force, the heart can turn our stories into "songs of freedom."

Final
Reflections

Nothing in the past can hurt us when we have learned a lesson from it. Nothing can happen in the future that is not happening now. Our job is to recognize in the present moment the peace and joy in our hearts.

THE LUCID DREAM

I was climbing a high mountain. Halfway to the top, it became slippery. I couldn't go any further. The dust fell all around me. I couldn't see anything. I was the only witness to my struggle.

My hands desperately tried to find something to hold on to, but the mountain was falling apart. So was I. In the midst of the end, I heard a voice singing,

You won't die, don't worry. Don't worry, you won't die.

I doubted the song. *But I'm about to!*

The song became louder and louder.

The song stopped abruptly. Just as I was about to fall, my hands found the roots of a tree. I held on to it. I was safe. The roots were part of a beautiful tree called Life.

The land disintegrated, and the dust fell on me, blinding my eyes. I could only hear the song. Doubt and fear made me wonder; I wondered about hope and love, wishing to understand life. In the end, it was all meant to be.

To climb the mountain, to struggle, to doubt, to fear, to hear the song, to hold on to the roots, to have faith, to love, to find the life that is always there, inside and outside the dream—this was what it all meant.

* * * *

The moment you choose to recognize your experiences in the world as lessons of love, life turns into a lucid dream. This recognition can come from the depths of your heart or from spiritual awareness through the senseless suffering caused by your mind. Either way, the main difference between a nightmare and a lucid dream is a shift of perception grounded in love. In the dream of life, there are many mountains to climb every day, and they might crumble, the dust might blur your vision, the fear might replace your hope, but if you have faith and recognize your own essence, you will never fall.

SHAKING OFF THE SAND

To write about something that is beyond thought is not possible; it can only be reduced to metaphors and stories of life-changing experiences, such as those found in these pages. I feel that a deep understanding of love, joy, and peace can only be known through our spiritual hearts. I was talking to a friend the other day when this metaphor came to me. I hope it resonates with you somehow. My friend seemed to understand, which filled me with joy.

I said to her, "Think of consciousness as an ocean that one day decided to experience itself as sand (symbolizing our bodies). It became drops of water covered by grains of sand. Now, if these drops of water were to look at each other, they would see grains of sand. Not knowing they are water in essence would allow them to fully experience what it is to be a grain of sand—to feel the wind transporting them from place to place, the sun turning them brown, the rubbing of their grains against each other, and so on. If the drops knew they were the ocean, this kind of interaction wouldn't happen. Think of enlightened people and how they lose interest in earthly things. These people know they are water and not sand, so their experience changes completely.

"Imagine all the droplets enjoying their experiences as sand, and then grains start to fall off, like in sickness, old age, or death. These droplets begin to see the water beneath the grains and recognize themselves as the ocean. In doing so, the droplets now live a different kind of experience; they know they are the ocean disguised as sand. As the sand continues to fall off, the droplets become more and more ocean-like. When the last grain of sand falls, the droplets happily return to their eternal essence. How interesting and amazing this would be!

"Now imagine what happens to droplets who still don't know they are the ocean, even when the sand starts to fall off. Fear sets in. In fear, the droplets grieve and suffer for every grain of sand they lose, especially when they witness other droplets losing theirs. Their belief that they are sand won't allow them to see the water underneath, even though it is right in front of them. These droplets remain on the shore for an unthinkable amount of time, covering themselves with new grains of sand. They can only reunite with the ocean when, though still covered in sand, they remember that they are water."

The mystery of life is beyond any metaphor, but recognizing a small fraction of the truth can liberate us from suffering, as Buddha once taught. There is a deeper knowing that connects suffering to love. All our physical and psychological pain are doorways to joy and peace. How is it possible not to see this?

Acknowledgments

It's with joy that I thank my mother, Valdeci Teles, for being my toughest spiritual teacher. I couldn't have learned as much as I did about forgiveness and compassion without her.

With deep gratitude, I thank Sherri Rowe for believing in me and in my message.

Much appreciation and respect for the editors of this manuscript: Laura Kenney, Kyra Hearn, Caitlin McKenna, Laura Shaine Cunningham, and Mary Ann Steinle.

A special thanks to all of my supporters whose names are too many to list here: Antonio Leite, Ann Procacci, Jaidev Alvarez, Kevin Forde, Nathalie LeBouler, Miguel Terc, Xavier Sabido, Edmund Kuuya, Betty Lou Leaver, Jo Anne Piccarillo, Fabiola Conceição, Vinka Pavelic, Amar Srivastava, Jennifer Lorino, Simone Valverdi, Liana Moraes, David Lillie, Ian Hurst, Adel Albuquerque, Milen Mirchev, Stephanie Wollenburg, Mark St. Germain, and all my social media friends.

With gratitude beyond words, I thank Christopher Terzakos, who came into my heart and life and contributed so much more joy.

Appendices

Appendix One

Conventional Fitness Program

In case you are wondering what my training routine and diet protocol were during my fittest years, I have included them here. These are strenuous workouts and restrictive meal plans that I used to follow; they are not a suggestion for you. If you are looking to lose weight, increase muscle mass, feel and look good, improve your energy, prevent disease, or improve your general health, this program might help. However, as you know by now, the meaning of being healthy goes beyond physical fitness. I believe that a truly healthy person is kind, and kindness comes from our spiritual hearts.

In the second appendix, I include the diet and training program I followed prior to competing. It's hard to believe I abused my body and mind to such levels. When memory brings back these life experiences, I often think of a blind person who stepped on other people's feet before they could see. The amazing thing about this life is that we can learn and change our lives in ways we never dreamed. It's certainly a radical change to be blind, then to be able to see again.

We are spiritual beings here to recognize, realize, and celebrate our true and loving nature, not to get lost further in pursuit of a fit and healthy body. Being in good shape and physically healthy can provide you with temporary happiness and well-being, but only a clear and peaceful mind can provide true satisfaction and joy.

Stephen Covey once said, "When man discovered the mirror, he lost his soul." I actually believe that we never lose our souls, we only temporarily replace them with attractive bodies.

However, I do believe that any physical activity can become a spiritual experience, even a tough type of training like weight lifting. The location where we train can become an open and auspicious terrain where spiritual and physical practices can be integrated. I feel this is important. In most commercial gyms, the weight lifting area is as far as we can get from spirituality. There is nothing there that reminds the mind and body that to be healthy is to be loving.

Weight lifting in commercial gyms can at best give us a feeling of being present in the moment, which is induced mostly by safety considerations—not meditation and active intention. Not only that, the owners and staff of such places are not intentionally aligned with the idea of offering both a physical and spiritual space for their customers. Most gyms are more preoccupied with counting their membership fees than with the well-being and happiness of our hearts.

TRAINING

Here is the training routine that I used for about two years before I competed with WBFF—World Beauty Fitness and Fashion. Weight lifting can be of great help with weight loss, staying in shape, and building strength, but as I have mentioned throughout this book, this type of training focuses only on the physical body, which is just one aspect of our being. We are so much more rich and complex than just our bodies! The approach to fitness that works the body in isolation from the mind and the spiritual heart is not what I do today, professionally or personally. My work at the moment is about integrating conventional physical fitness with spirituality.

The workout plans here are only to illustrate what my journey was like. They are not approved recommendations.

Monday

- Legs and Glutes (3 sets of 8: 12 reps)
- Core and glute activation warm-up (plank / spider plank / glute bridge)
- Barbell squats
- Deadlift
- Jump squats
- Walking lunges
- Kettlebell swing
- Glute kickbacks
- Bulgarian split squat
- Dumbbell step-up
- Smith machine calf raise
- Leg press

Tuesday

- Back Biceps—Abs (3 sets of 8: 12 reps)
- Warm-up (wall angels / resistance band stretch)
- Lat pull down (wide and chin-up grip)
- Chin-ups / Pull-ups
- Seated row
- Lat pull straight bar
- Barbell bent-over row
- Renegade rows
- Dumbbell curls
- Reverse rows supine
- Abs: cable rotation, reverse crunches, and hanging leg raise

Wednesday

- Chest—Triceps (3 sets of 8: 12 reps)
- Floor push-up
- Incline push-up
- Cable fly
- Barbell bench press
- Dumbbell flies
- Dip
- Dumbbell pullovers
- Cable triceps
- Plate front press

Thursday

- Legs and Glutes (3 sets of 8: 12 reps)
- Core and glute activation warm-up (plank / spider plank / glute bridge)
- Barbell squats
- Deadlift
- Jump squats
- Walking lunges
- Kettlebell swing
- Glute kickbacks
- Bulgarian split squat
- Dumbbell step-up
- Smith machine calf raise
- Leg press

Friday

- Shoulders, Chest, and Abs (3 sets of 8: 12 reps)
- Push-ups
- Cable fly
- Barbell bench press
- Dumbbell flies
- Dip
- Barbell shoulder press
- Front and lateral raise
- Dumbbell shoulder press—alternating
- Battling ropes
- Farmer's walk, plus shrugs
- Abs: reverse crunches, hanging leg raise, knee/hip raise

Saturday

- Full Body—Crossfit Style (1 hour, 30 minutes—1 minute per exercise)
- Push-ups
- Box jump
- Treadmill sprints
- Chin-ups
- Tire flip
- Burpee
- Jump rope
- Dips

Sunday

- Active Rest
- 45-minute walk and foam rolling

Important Note: The workout plans here are only to illustrate what my journey was like. They are not approved recommendations.

DIET

These meal suggestions are only to illustrate what my personal journey was like. They are not approved meal-plan recommendations.

Breakfast Option One
- 8 oz cold water with probiotic supplement
- 1 tablespoon matcha green tea + ½ lemon
- 7 walnuts
- 1-2 whole eggs

Breakfast Option Two
- 1 salmon filet oven-roasted in coconut oil
- 5-10 walnuts
- Steamed kale

Breakfast Option Three
- Steel-cut oats, almond milk, berries
- Green tea

Lunch
- Any lean meat of your choice: white fish (sole, cod, flounder, or halibut), grass-fed red meat, tuna fish, wild salmon, chicken breast, turkey breast, sardines in water
- Eat with steamed veggies or a green salad
- Avoid sauces; instead, use olive oil, apple cider vinegar, and avocado oil for salad dressing

Snack - Best Options
- 1 tablespoon spirulina shake with ½ oz. frozen organic berries and a teaspoon of coconut oil
- Green juice (no fruit added)
- Protein shake (whey protein)
- Nuts (walnuts, macadamias, pecans, Brazil nuts)
- Raw coconut flakes
- Celery, cucumber, or carrots with almond butter
- Kale chips or dried seaweed
- Raw cheese (unpasteurized)
- Sweet potato chips (homemade)

Dinner
- The same options as lunch
- Important to AVOID:
  - Alcohol
  - All sugar and sweets
  - Regular fruit except for berries and green apples
  - Starchy carbs such as pasta, bread, rice, wheat wraps, white potatoes, etc.

Drinks
- Water
- Kombucha
- All kinds of tea, but especially green tea, no sugar added
- Coffee (no sugar added)

Other Details
- Sleep 8 hours or more per night
- Drink a gallon of water a day as well as green tea
- All vegetables and fruit should be organic
- Adding lemon to your meals is great—it alkalizes the body
- You can have a small piece of dark chocolate 85% cacao or higher, but not every day
- Use stevia powder as the only sweetener

Grocery List
This list was on my phone for so long that I should know it by heart now, and sort of do. Here it goes:
- Organic eggs
- Meats: chicken breast, lean beef, turkey breast
- Seafood: salmon, sardines, mackerel
- Cottage cheese
- Fat-free Greek yogurt
- Grass-fed butter
- Coconut oil
- Olive oil
- Flavorings and condiments that do not contain sugars and preservatives or vegetable seed oils

Important Note: These meal suggestions are only to illustrate what my personal journey was like. They are not approved meal-plan recommendations.

- Almonds
- Flaxseeds
- Pumpkin seeds
- Sunflower seeds
- Brazil nuts
- Macadamia nuts
- Walnuts
- Stevia powder
- Green leafy vegetables (spinach, cabbage, lettuces, etc.)
- Asparagus
- Avocados
- Cucumber
- Carrots
- Broccoli
- Brussels sprouts
- Lemon
- Cabbage
- Sweet potatoes
- Celery
- Onions
- Garlic
- Peppers
- Sauerkraut
- Tomatoes
- Fresh and frozen berries
- Matcha green tea
- Almond milk
- Apple cider vinegar
- Spirulina
- Steel-cut oats
- Ezekiel sprouted bread
- Whey protein
- Raw cheese

Supplements
- Multivitamin
- B complex
- D3
- Krill oil
- Green powder
- CoQ10

Important Note: These meal suggestions are only to illustrate what my personal journey was like. They are not approved meal-plan recommendations.

WEIGHT LOSS SPIRITUAL INSIGHT

Most of us know that the best way to lose weight is to eat less, especially foods that are high in fats such as nuts, full-fat dairy products, avocados, oils, etc. Healthy fats are better for our overall health. Sugar is another well-known adversary of weight loss. But before depriving yourself of healthy fats and all sweets, try eating half of what you normally eat. Next time you weigh yourself, you will likely be surprised. In my experience, there can be a struggle to eat less when oftentimes we feel like eating more. I know this to be true because the presence of hope and fear is deeply and subconsciously operating in our minds. Food is one of many people's biggest addictions, stemming as it does from our emotional triggers, which are linked to all kinds of insecurities.

The more hope we have for a better future, and the more we fear not achieving what we expect or want, the more we eat. Hope and fear take us away from this moment, which is perfect just the way it is. Here and now, there is enough space to embrace everything that is happening without creating unnecessary escapes into the past and future. Escaping into the past and future was the motivation that made chocolate bars a part of my diet for a while. It was a response to all kinds of hope I had, while exercising hard at the gym was a response to my fear and guilt over eating chocolate, and as a result of not pleasing others with my image.

We tend to be either in the past or in the future, when in truth, we would benefit greatly from being in the present moment. When we are in the moment, we relax and merge with our surroundings and experiences; there is no anxiety there, just peace and even bliss.

We hope to be happy and peaceful one day being in a perfect romantic relationship, or making great money doing what we love, or having loyal friends—among a long list of other feel-good things, both material and immaterial. In my case, I not only feared not having these things, I also tried really hard to hide that I didn't have them, or pretended I was okay with it so others would accept me as a positive and inspirational person. As you now know,

I've gotten myself into all kinds of "healthy" addictions to hide my hopes and fears; fitness was one of them.

To make these points even clearer, I will put it this way. I find that there are two simple practices we can engage in to live a real, healthy life aimed toward body-mind harmony. One is to give up hope and replace it with aspiration or motivation from the heart—that is, to stop waiting to be happy when something happens, and to instead rejoice in this very moment for doing what you do, because what you are doing now should already be the realization of what you want to happen in the future. Think about the aspiration to be happy in a romantic relationship, for instance. It's a wonderful thing, but if we are not happy with ourselves the way we are now, there isn't anyone in the world—or beyond—who will make us happy. So the idea behind replacing hope with aspiration in your heart is to think of external things as triggers for more happiness to come into your heart, not the reasons for your core happiness, because you've got this basic covered.

The other way toward body-mind harmony is to go beyond fear. This may be harder than the first practice, simply because most of us are very good at closing down and deceiving ourselves with the idea that we are okay with what we have, when in truth, we are not. It's incredible—our ability to hurt ourselves by ignoring our deepest desires in the attempt to suffer less. In fact, we are living in denial of our own nature, inclinations, conditionings, and uniqueness. This is where going beyond fear comes into play, to bring our being to full expression in this lifetime.

The non-intellectual, straightforward way of putting it is to simply accept yourself the way you are, where you are. Most of the time, we fear letting ourselves just "be" because we believe that there is no space big enough in the universe for us to "stretch" to our full being. We feel that it might be too embarrassing or awkward to do that. So we constrict ourselves into our little mental room of fear and stay there. This is the story of my life. I spent almost all my life in this room of fear—to the point that I entertained suicidal thoughts.

The technique I now use to "stretch" myself and go beyond the fear is to make the external room larger and larger. Being mindful and aware is very important to this process. First, you must learn how to detect and acknowledge the perceptions and emotions that make you feel small and constricted; then, you must find your own way to let those feelings and emotions pass through you without getting stuck in your rational mind. This does not in any way mean ignoring these feelings; we are simply giving them room to expand to the point of passing through the body and mind without staying there. So what we are doing is welcoming the energies that are attracted to our bodies and minds; this way, they don't become hostile. Think of finding yourself face to face with a well-fed wild animal. We are only in danger if we try to defend ourselves by attacking the animal or trying to run from it. If we can relax and share the space with this well-fed animal (energy), it won't cause us any harm. The opposite is likely to happen—we'll learn to enjoy ourselves around well-fed wild animals (powerful energies), and this can create an instant, body-mind harmony experience. Going beyond fear simply means fully embracing and welcoming the energies that come to visit our bodies and minds in a specific moment. By this, I don't mean either rejecting these energies or acting upon them when it is not appropriate or healthy, but rather recognizing their presence and letting them be. Our rational minds are very good at trying to take control of the natural and spontaneous energies of our bodies and minds (thoughts), in some way or another. Ultimately, this attempt to control causes disharmony between the body and mind.

In conclusion, there is no better way to lose weight than dropping hopes and fears. Engaging in this practice will likely cause us to enjoy and appreciate ourselves just the way we are, by helpinng us realize that the idea of looking thin was just another way to please and live for others while hurting ourselves. Although being thin can be healthier, remember tip number one about hope: when we are already happy, to be happier is a gift coming from the aspirations of the heart.

Appendix Two

Diet and Training Program for Competitors

The information below is only meant to illustrate what extreme diets and exercise programs for competitors look like. I do not recommend that anyone follow this kind of program, first because I am not a nutritionist, and second because I no longer believe in practicing extreme behaviors to achieve physical health.

A meal plan for a competition is not structured the way a regular diet plan is (i.e., divided into sections such as breakfast, morning snack, lunch, afternoon snack, and dinner). Here, it's all about meal frequency and portion size in addition to food selection. You must eat every two to three hours. It's a diet designed to regulate blood sugar, which could help diabetic or pre-diabetic people; however, the best way to know what diet is good for you is to consult your nutritionist and listen to your body.

These meal suggestions are only to illustrate what my personal journey was like. They are not approved recommendations.

Introduction

This diet didn't change much. I was on it for a few months.

- 8 oz warm lemon water; 15 minutes later, 10 oz water with green powdered wheat grass with collagen and probiotics
- Meal 1: 1 whole egg and 3 egg whites with veggies and a small piece of avocado
- Meal 2: 4 oz chicken breast and green beans or spinach
- Meal 3: egg-white omelet (6 eggs, bell pepper, spinach, tomatoes, 1 tablespoon of unsweetened almond milk), or cottage cheese, or fat-free Greek yogurt with 2 scoops of whey protein
- Meal 4: 4 oz salmon and green beans
- Meal 5: 2 oz sirloin steak with bok choy
- 2 cups of matcha green tea throughout the day between meals
- 1 gallon of water
- No cheat meals

Diet Information

Recommendations and tips from my competition coach at the time.

- Amount to eat is based on food category per meal: fibrous vegetables unlimited; protein, 4 oz for meat, fat-free cheese or soy products; 4 egg whites; and half-cup for non-fat dairy
- Fruit only after workout (no juice)
- Fibrous vegetables are great since they don't raise insulin. The problem with raising insulin is that protein should be eaten in combination with fibrous vegetables; for example, Brussels sprouts and chicken without the skin, broccoli and sirloin beef.
- Avoid tropical and dry fruits
- Go with egg whites instead of whole eggs
- Avoid nuts, nut butter, and edamame
- Whey protein powder, egg white protein, rice, and hemp were fine, but they needed to contain 2g or less of carbs and sugar
- All dairy should be fat-free

Important Note: These meal suggestions are only to illustrate what my personal journey was like. They are not approved recommendations.

- Low-carb, gluten-free bread
- The only starchy foods allowed are quinoa, barley, red beans, black-eyed peas, lima beans, black beans, adzuki, chick peas, corn, carrots, peas, popcorn, acorn squash, spaghetti, butternut squash, lentils, split peas, millet, bulgur, bran, low-carb wraps and breads, low-carb pasta
- Protein bars: only Quest, Oh Yea Victory, paleo bars, and Lift
- Eat sparingly: carrots, beets, and onions—they have too much sugar
- Fats allowed in small amounts: olive oil, coconut oil, unsweetened coconut flakes, avocado, pine nuts, pumpkin seeds
- Coffee and matcha green tea are diuretic—they help reduce water weight
- Best lean proteins: chicken breast, egg whites, white turkey breast, white fish, flounder, halibut, tilapia, bass, sole, cod, sardines in water, extra-firm tofu, and tempeh
- Best fatty proteins: salmon, swordfish, mackerel, Chilean sea bass, red meat, bison, whole eggs, soft tofu, lamb, and pork
- Best dairy proteins: plain Greek yogurt, fat-free cottage cheese, fat-free ricotta cheese, fat-free cheese
- Best veggies: green beans and asparagus because they are diuretic, which helps reduce water weight; all the cruciferous veggies are also great
- Condiments allowed: soy sauce and tamari, Dijon mustard, balsamic vinegar and other vinegars, dried herbs, hot sauce, salt, ginger, garlic, and stevia
- Recommend low-carb protein powders, such as Isopure
- Avoid diet sodas; drink more green tea instead
- Eliminate all juices, alcohol, and sodas
- Take vitamin C, 500mg twice a day
- Take probiotic, refrigerated, a.m. and p.m.
- Recommend BCAA before and after workouts
- Do not eat out of containers—always put food in a bowl and measure it

Important Note: These meal suggestions are only to illustrate what my personal journey was like. They are not approved recommendations.

- Get a food scale
- To reduce water weight, take dandelion root pills
- Drink green tea or coffee, pre-workout or cardio
- The goal was to get 30-35 grams of protein per meal; some basic guidelines were: 6 egg whites, or 1 cup of cottage cheese, or 4.5 oz of lean meat, or 5 oz of fish

The Supplements

- Multivitamin (to make sure I was getting all the nutrients my body needed for muscle building and strength)
- Vitamin D3 5000 (bone and skin health, helps with the absorption of calcium)
- CoQ10 (antioxidant—energy and cell growth booster)
- Resveratrol (antioxidant—energy booster, protects the body against cancer and heart diseases)
- Collagen Booster (to tighten up the skin and promote joint health)
- Krill Oil (antioxidant with omega 3 fatty acids; helps to lower triglyceride levels)
- Probiotic for women (improve digestion - nutrient absorption)
- Calm Magnesium raspberry-lemon (to decrease production of stress hormones)
- Amazing Grass green wheat grass powder (a vitamin and mineral supplement)
- Matcha green tea (to boost metabolism)
- Organic whey protein (to help with muscle building)
- Vitamin C (antioxidant—iron absorption)
- Vitamin B6 (helps the body metabolize fats and protein— also good for energy)
- Tribulus terrestris herbal supplement (improves cardiovascular health and circulation)
- Yohimbine HCl (increases fat loss)
- DIM—Diindolymethane—naturally found in Cruciferous vegetables (prevents drastic increases or decreases in estrogen)
- Vitamin B12 (to give extra energy)

Important Note: These meal suggestions are only to illustrate what my personal journey was like. They are not approved recommendations.

- True Athlete Creatinine (5g before weights for muscle endurance)
- DHEA 50g (first thing in the morning, helps to build muscle)
- BCAAs (before and after workout, helps maintain muscle mass while on a low-carb diet)

The Training
- Cardio: 45 minutes to 1 hour walking on treadmill fully inclined at a speed of 2.5 mph, five days per week (Not on an empty stomach as my coach had suggested.)
- Weights: I focused on compound exercises. These are exercises that recruit two or more different joints to activate a whole muscle group. I also performed isolating exercises. I didn't follow a specific order, but kept the same muscle group exercises in sequence.

Day 1: Chest/Shoulders/Triceps (sets of 3)
- Barbell bench press: 105 lbs. / 6-8 reps
- Floor push-ups: 15-20 reps
- Dumbbell flies: 20 lbs. / 10-12 reps
- Dumbbell bench press: 25-30 lbs. / 10-12 reps
- Barbell incline bench press: 85 lbs. / 8-10 reps
- Leverage incline chest press: 40 lbs. / 10-12 reps
- Standing military press: 75-85 lbs. / 8-10 reps
- Arnold press: 25-30 lbs. / 8-10 reps
- Dumbbell front raise: 15 lbs. / 8-10 reps
- Plate front raise: 25-35 lbs. / 8-10 reps
- Dumbbell side lateral raise: 15 lbs. / 8-10 reps
- Dumbbell rear lateral raise: 15 lbs. / 8-10 reps
- Barbell rear delt row: 65-75 lbs. / 8-10 reps
- Dumbbell single raise: 20-25 lbs. / 8-10 reps
- Bodyweight dips: 8-10 reps
- Dip machine: 75-90 lbs. / 10-12 reps
- Triceps pushdown with rope: 25-30 lbs. / 8-10 reps
- Plate shrug: 45 lbs. / 12-15 reps

Important Note: These meal suggestions are only to illustrate what my personal journey was like. They are not approved recommendations.

Day 2: Back & Biceps (sets of 3)

- Bent-over rows: 65-75 lbs. / 10-12 reps
- Reverse rows—bodyweight: 10-12 reps
- Single-arm dumbbell rows: 35-40 lbs. / 10-12 reps
- Front lat pulldowns: 75-85 lbs. / 10-12 reps
- Bodyweight chin-ups: 10-15 reps
- Bodyweight pull-ups: 3-5 reps
- Seated cable rows (wide and close grip): 75-85 lbs. / 10-12 reps
- Hyperextensions: 10-15 reps
- Hammer curls: 20 lbs. / 10-12 reps
- Biceps curls: 20-25 lbs. / 10-12 reps
- Ez bar curls: 50-60 lbs. / 10-12 reps
- Overhead cable curls: 15 lbs. each side / 10-12 reps

Day 3: Legs & Quads (sets of 3)

- Barbell back squat: 135-155 lbs. / 8-10 reps
- Barbell front squat: 115-135 lbs. / 8-10 reps
- Barbell box squat: 135 lbs. / 10-12 reps
- Leg press: 270-360 lbs. / 8-10 reps
- Walking lunges: 40-50 lbs. / 15-25 steps
- Dumbbell step-up: 30-40 lbs. / 15-20 reps
- Kettlebell goblet squat: 50 lbs. / 15-20 reps
- Bodyweight pistol squat: 8-10 reps
- Calf press: 90 lbs. / 15-20 reps

Day 4: Abs & Arms (sets of 3)

- Dumbbell overhead triceps press: 20-25 lbs. / 10-12 reps
- Triceps pushdown: 25-30 lbs. / 10-12 reps
- Bench dips: 10-12 reps
- Bodyweight dips: 10-12 reps
- Plank hold: 1-2 minutes
- Spider plank: 20-25 reps
- Hanging leg raises: 20-25 reps
- Reverse crunches: 20-25 reps
- Ab roller: 20-25 reps
- Cable rotation: 15-20 lbs. / 20-25 reps

Important Note: These meal suggestions are only to illustrate what my personal journey was like. They are not approved recommendations.

- Dumbbell curl: 20 lbs. / 8-10 reps
- Dumbbell lateral raise: 15 lbs. / 8-10 reps
- Dumbbell front raise: 15 lbs. / 8-10 reps
- Bodyweight chin-ups: 10-15 reps

Day 5: Glutes & Hamstrings (sets of 3)

- Barbell deadlift: 135-155 lbs. / 10-12 reps
- Stiff-legged deadlifts: 135 lbs. / 10-12 reps
- Sumo deadlift: 135 lbs. / 10-12 reps
- Kettlebell single leg deadlift: 50 lbs. / 10-12 reps
- Bench sand bag & plate hip thrusts: 70-80 lbs. / 10-12 reps
- Glute bridge: 10-12 reps
- Crab walk: 1-2 minutes
- Dumbbell Bulgarian split squats: 30 lbs. / 10-12 reps
- Cable kickback: 25-30 lbs. / 10-12 reps
- Smith machine single-leg step-up: 50-60 lbs.
- Lying leg curl: 70 lbs. / 10-12 reps
- Hyperextensions: 12-15 reps

Day 6: Total Body (sets of 3)

- Kettlebell swing: 15- 20 reps
- Around-the-world lunges: 10-12 reps each direction
- Battle rope: to failure
- Tire flipping: to failure
- Jump rope: to failure
- Burpees: to failure
- Jumping squats: to failure
- Walkouts with a push-up: 15- 20 reps
- Treadmill sprints: 30 seconds

Important Note: These meal suggestions are only to illustrate what my personal journey was like. They are not approved recommendations.

THE END

The end is never the end when we live from the heart.

www.FITFORJOY.org

Much Love.

About the Author

Valeria Teles is a certified personal trainer, winning fitness competitor, author, and the creator of the Fit for Joy philosophy. Born in Brazil, she began her professional career in the arts, both music and dance, before finding her way to fitness. With more than twenty years in the fitness industry, Valeria has designed the Fit for Joy wellness center project to instruct others in her method of maintaining a joyful life. She is currently devoted to writing and hosting the Fit for Joy gatherings.

KIND HEARTS - STRONG BODIES - PEACEFUL MINDS

WWW.FITFORJOY.ORG